Marks of an Unwanted Rainbow

by Paul Yusuf McCormack

Kirwin Maclean
Associates

First published in 2022
Kirwin Maclean Associates
4 Mesnes Green,
Lichfield Staffordshire
WS14 9AB

Graphic design by Tora Kelly
Photography mostly by Joanne Roebuck
Cover photo used with the kind premission of Andrew Fox
Editing by Siobhan Maclean and Joanne Roebuck
Printed and bound 4edge, Essex

ISBN - 978-1912130542

Contents

Looking Back

My Mother and Me

Preface

I was once asked about childhood...what should it look like?
It's a difficult one to respond to but, I guess ultimately, it should be a safe place where a child can grow, be nurtured, acknowledged, encouraged, accepted, loved and mostly happy.

Unfortunately, for some children this isn't the case and circumstances out of their control can take over, leaving childhood as a word which holds very little meaning for them.

Mine was such a childhood. Adversity, violence and abuse 'flavoured' it and marked many of my milestones.

I grew up in children's institutions during the mid 1960s and 70s. These weren't the safest places for any child to grow up in, more so when illegitimacy, being coloured and religious doctrine were mixed together. My childhood, therefore, became a scary place. I didn't know or understand why I was in a children's home. All I knew was that I wasn't wanted or like other children, and these points were referenced continuously to me, which only confirmed the feelings I held about myself.

In 2015, aged 52, I wrote a small verse that summed up my childhood life when I was 5 years old. It describes how I felt after a particularly harrowing beating where I'd been stripped to my pants, dragged by my hair to the workroom upstairs by the Sister in charge, a room where clothes were repaired and mended, but never little children. The cane was wielded in a brutal fashion, indiscriminately striking the flesh of my near naked body, and words and names were screamed at me, striking me just as hard.

After the punishment ceased, I was further dragged to the cloister, a pitch-black corridor, and made to kneel. Instructions were barked and I was told to pray to God for the forgiveness of me. I knelt there, struggling to contemplate all my many sins and why I was so bad, I didn't understand my life, nor why I hurt so much inside. I only ever wanted someone to be kind to me, even if it was only for one day. It is in this quiet moment where the following poem lives:

A Butterfly's Heartbeat

It's quiet now.
The world has stopped,
Just for a moment.

I can lick my wounds,
They're only on the surface,
They will heal.

Inside it's harder.
The wounds are deeper,
I can't always reach them,
Only feel them,
They carry so much pain.

Listen! I mean really listen....
Sometimes you can hear the beat
Of a butterfly's heart.

Focus,
Take,
Remove yourself from your body.

I hadn't cried since I was 6 years of age, but tears began to fall, and my body let out a 'noise'. It went into its own primal grief, shaking, control no longer mine. The child that was me screamed at the life we shared, the horror, the helplessness, the fear of being unloved and being so unlovable.

This continued for two days. I was unable to stop the surges of tears and pain, but I knew that I needed to console my inner child if I was going to get through this. Fatigue took over and I came to a decision: To write the words down; to let me, the child, speak; to let me say everything in my head and heart; to let me say what I witnessed. And so, I began writing. I became possessed and wrote reams and reams of words mixed with my tears.

Approximately 18 months later I decided to use my words to explore. This book is a collection of 52 poems. Each one represents and marks the 52 years it took the child in me to find 'our' voice.

What I do know is this, my childhood shaped me, but I haven't let it define me. I choose who I want to be.

The Boy who Became a Giant

Siobhan Maclean

Paul was many things to many people. He had many names and when he died, he was yet to decide exactly how to use his names as the author of this book. Sometimes he used initials for Paul or for Yusuf – Paul Y or P Yusuf; sometimes he used brackets for some of his names Paul Yusuf (McCormack) or Yusuf (Paul) McCormack. To me Paul was always Paul. The card he sent to me days before he died said 'with love from Paul' as everything from him did. I have toyed with how to refer to this giant of a man through this book and have opted for Paul.

I first met Paul early in 2016. He sent me an email introducing himself as a foster carer who wanted to write something. Apparently, the social worker leading his 'men in foster care' group had mentioned me, shown him one of my books and suggested he get in touch. To be honest, I just didn't have the time to talk to someone about their writing. I had not long returned to work following a significant stroke which had resulted in me needing to relearn to read and write. Reading now takes real energy and I had decided that I would focus on reading only what was essential for my work. At that stage, for a range of reasons, I didn't tell people about the impact the stroke had had on my reading and how debilitating stroke fatigue is. I decided not to explain my reasoning but tried to send a kind email wishing him well and providing names of people Paul might want to contact. Thankfully, Paul didn't take my gentle 'no' for an answer. So, we met and talked.

Paul came to see me at my home. I can still remember when he arrived and am writing through tears now thinking about the man that I met and the journey we went on together. Paul was physically a big guy, but as soon as I opened the door, I saw a young boy looking back at me. I don't know if it was something in Paul's eyes or the satchel that he was literally clutching which gave me that impression, but that sense of a child standing in front of me in a man's body towering over me was key to the start of our relationship. We spent hours together just talking and I knew then that we would go on a journey together.

Paul had started to write about his childhood, and he wanted to develop his writing. In that first meeting he told me a little about his childhood experiences, but mostly outlined his dream. He was now a foster carer and could see that whilst social work had moved on there were still things that really bothered him about social workers' practice. He had started to get involved in a local social work qualifying course, but he wanted to do more to change the experience of children. Paul had read some of my books and he asked if I would mentor him as he developed his own writing.

In the years since then Paul and I have met regularly, away from view. Our relationship was profoundly important to me, and I grew to love Paul. We usually met at my house (I even have a small pot of sugar that has 'Paul's sugar' written on it – no one at home has sugar but I've not been able to get rid of it). Sometimes we ate out. We have enjoyed many of Lichfield's eateries together and laughed about how we could become food critics. If we weren't eating out Paul always brought cake. He wrecked my diet plans often (but I learnt that sharing a meal and gifts of food was an important part of Paul's relationships with others). I mentored Paul as he had asked me, but he became my mentor and confidante too. We shared many reflections, and he was always my first 'go to' to discuss anything about children and social care. Even now, something will happen and I think "*I must ask Paul what he thinks…*" then I catch my breath.

I was involved in developing the SHARE model for social work with Jo Finch and Prospera Tedam. Paul supported us in developing and testing the model and he contributed to the book about the model published in 2018. We had a book launch very early in 2018 which turned out to be a bit of a disaster as there was a dreadful snowstorm so very few people came – but Paul travelled all the way to London, walking from the station because there was no other transport, to read one of his poems. Paul was hugely committed to SHARE. He believed in the importance of connecting seeing, hearing, action, reading and evaluation in the work that we do with children. Later that year I was invited to do some videos for a collection that Sage were putting together about social work theory. They wanted me talk about reflective practice, and I suggested that SHARE would work well and asked if Paul could come. We had a brilliant day filming (food was involved of course) and the team were so impressed with Paul that they asked him to do a film on his own too. He stepped up and did a brilliant film about being a 'child of the state', mentioning his work on this book.

When I was asked to develop a workbook for social workers working with children and families, I knew immediately I wanted Paul to be involved. Paul contributed such a lot to that workbook writing 'Paul's Perspective' in each chapter. The workbook is still a popular resource and so many people tell me how much they have learnt from Paul through that book. The cover of the book was Paul's artwork. This piece holds personal meaning for me because Paul developed it following one of our regular meetings. He sent me photos of it in various stages and told me about the different ways in which it represented our relationship. We took that picture to a number of events where we were both speaking and sometimes asked people to write down what they thought it meant. We pulled together the responses and had plans to do something with them exploring the link between art appreciation and the development of analytical skills in social workers. We still had so much to do together.

Paul and I spoke together at a number of World Social Work Day events from Cardiff to Chester. I remember how much time and thought he put into those events. World Social Work Day is always the third Tuesday in March – it often falls very close to St Patricks Day and Paul talked about the irony of this often. You will see why when you read 'Cake for Tea'. Paul created some beautiful pieces of art to share with social workers encouraging them to put the love into social work. He spent hours on those. I sometimes wonder if students and social workers listening to him on World Social Work Day understood the value of the gift that Paul was giving to them. In the last few years Paul worked with his 'soul sister' Saira-Jayne (with whom he set up 'Artifacts') on World Social Work Day. His final World Social Work Day, into which he had put so much thought, was prevented by Covid restrictions and we talked about the loss he felt. I remember saying that there would be lots of other World Social Work Days but there was no other World Social Work Day for Paul and it will never be the same for me again.

Post Covid lockdown our meetings continued, but now they were online. We learnt together how to navigate the new world of zoom meetings. I remember with laughter now the first zoom meeting we had and the number of messages between us and a couple of phone calls to make it work, but I also remember how 'safe' I felt in what was then a very lonely and uncertain world when Paul's face appeared on screen and the audio connected with his wonderfully gentle voice. That's why I want you, the reader, to see Paul's face and hear his voice as part of your experience. So, on page 194 I have included a selection of Paul's work. If you follow the QR codes, they will take you to a treasure of photographic, video and audio material which captures some of Paul's body of work. I felt it was important to include these codes as we had talked about Paul doing some videos specifically to go with the book which we could include as QR codes. Paul would often combine his spoken word performance with his art at his exhibitions and we had wanted to capture the feelings that standing in front of Paul's art and hearing his words evoked.

When we first met, Paul had only recently started writing and yet he had reams of material. He started to further communicate his experiences through art after we met. Paul was a prolific artist and although he had only recently started to paint and create, he leaves behind an amazing body of work. His art and poetry connected in many ways, but there was also a key difference. A central part of his poetry and spoken word performances was the 'preambles' which to a large extent provided an explanation and context of the work, but Paul rarely titled his art and never gave a detailed explanation, instead he wanted to know what people saw in it.

"What I understand about art is this, it's a way of expressing how we feel. There isn't a right or wrong image. It is the creator's message that says what they see or feel. How others interpret it, is largely based on their own life experiences and ideas at that time. So, to me art, is another way of communicating." (McCormack 2019:243)

We often saw Paul's art in different ways and what started as a quick conversation about a piece of art could develop into hours of face-to-face discussion, followed up with some phone messages and a couple of emails. We both loved the phrase often attributed to Anaïs Nin "We don't see things as they are, we see them as we are."

We had agreed that in this book that we would include the narratives which went with each poem (see pages 154 - 174) but that the art would not have the same contextual explanation. Instead, we had agreed that we would each write something about some of the underlying themes in the art. Here Paul thought that we would bring together our very different voices around social work with children and families. My voice as a social worker and Paul's voice with his various hats as a 'child of the state', foster carer and social work trainer. This was really all we had left to do on the book when Paul died. Many times, since his death I have sat down to pull this book together and I have been through a range of emotions which have led to a range of actions. For a long time, I struggled to read beyond the second verse of 'My Voice, Our Voice' the first poem in the collection (you will see why when you read it). I have cried, I have shouted, I have avoided the tasks. I have sat for hours just thinking, I have frenetically scrawled through thousands of emails and messages between us.

Even now, I don't know whether to include my thoughts about the underlying themes in the art. I am writing here, but it may not make the final cut of the book. Paul wanted this, so I should include it. But it would have sat alongside Paul's thoughts, so I shouldn't include it… I have some of Paul's thoughts that I can draw on, but I know this part of the book would have been so much stronger had he been here.

There are a number of themes to Paul's art:

Labels: Perhaps the most well-known piece of Paul's artwork is 'No Colours for my Coat.' This is one of the first pieces he worked on. Here is something Paul wrote about creating the piece.

"This particular piece of work started life as a short verse titled No Colours for my Coat and I wondered if I could draw something that represented what I was trying to say. It became an awakening of me the artist, allowing my

suppressed creativity a voice! After I'd sketched out a small doodle I thought 'Could I make a jacket?' Six weeks later I'd finished, and I stood back. The enormity of what I'd done struck me. Emotionally I still get tearful when I look at this piece of work. How could such a little boy be so deserving of the toxicity and hatred thrown at him? To be viewed as worthless, less than others, whilst subjected to daily taunts and expressions from those who were supposed to be caring for you is difficult. It challenges one's belief in humanity and whether kindness exists. Life was tough, I hoped each morning that I'd either be dead or that someone would stand up for me today...It didn't happen. The work represents my 'life story' of growing up in care... words, expressions, sayings, a total of 337 labels attributed to me (and I never asked for any). The buff labels represent the daily onslaught. Black labels become the words I took to my heart and flowed through my very core, they become my belief system and how I valued myself. The coloured labels are some of the things I wanted people to see. I wanted people to know that I could be a good boy, that I wasn't full of badness or evil, that I believed in kindness and that someone could like or maybe love me...not big asks really!"

Labels become a core theme in much of Paul's work. To prepare for the publication of this book, we worked (virtually) together during the first lockdown on creating a video which Paul titled "Labels are for Tins not People." That is the simplicity of the message. The complexity, that we often discussed and debated, is the fact that people will always carry labels of some kind, but social workers need to support children and their families to create and carry positive labels which they select for themselves.

Words: Paul includes words on lots of his paintings and every label used in his work contains words. I went to see Paul's first exhibition with Rosie, my youngest daughter, just before she went off to university. We have enjoyed going to art exhibitions together many times, but few have prompted so much discussion afterwards (and still does more than three years later). Rosie had never even heard some of the words included in Paul's work. Horrible nasty words. The three of us reflected on this together and the fact that even though some words have been effectively 'banned in polite society' the words that are attached to some children now can be as powerfully undermining. Students just starting social work training now may be the same age as Rosie and they need to 'hear' some of those words which they may never have heard. Most importantly they need the opportunity to reflect on how some of the words in common use now might be viewed in 30 years' time. That is what Paul's work brings to us all. Paul's work is not about the history of social work with children and families. This is about the past, the present and very much the future.

Jigsaw pieces: In social work we often talk about gathering all the pieces of information in a situation and putting this together like a jigsaw puzzle. Paul told me that, in his view, this missed the point. What about helping the child put their own jigsaw together? Whilst Paul didn't often title his artwork the piece included on page 89 was called 'the puzzlement of me'. This is what Paul said about the painting:

"Not understanding or being told why you're in care rattled around in my head a lot as a child. I had no concept of why I was there… I believed that I was so bad that no one could ever want me. Care is a lonely place for any child, and I carried these feelings and those of isolation and not belonging with me each day. Because of the negativity hurled at me, I didn't hold myself with any regard. I desperately wanted those who were in charge of me, as well as my teachers, my social workers, the good people of the parish, the day kids…basically I wanted everyone to see something 'good' in me. This picture represents the way I wanted or thought about myself, my identity if you like. I didn't know who I was or more importantly who I could be. I didn't understand the rhetoric and jibes especially those with a racial slant. My 'Puzzlement' is exactly that, some pieces are the parts of me that are aspirational (they were the things I thought I was good at and would say to people 'This is what I'm about'), whilst others are those that I clung onto with a desperation, I needed to believe goodness resided in me. (As a small child I was asked what I wanted to be when I was big, "A kind boy" was my response, I knew it must exist, my conflict was at odds because of the actions of others). The colours show the positivity of my ideas about what or who I am and the missing piece…Well, it's the missed opportunities that could have given me my sense of identity, my story, the reasons for me being where I was, the reasons for why I remained…. The not knowing meant I was troubled emotionally and often communicated through angry displays and altercations…Interestingly my file even notes this, aged 14 and a half, after asking, I was given some information. It states 'he received the information without batting an eyelid. It seems to have had a calming effect and he no longer appears angry'… (There's a lesson here!)"

Everyone has the right to have all the pieces of their puzzle. Paul and I often talked about the number of care experienced adults receiving their 'files' with nothing but redacted information in them. Paul wanted social workers to know that everyone needs all the pieces. Don't keep the jigsaw puzzle to yourself!

Paul had more highly developed skills in reflexivity and analysis than most people I know. We often talked about the fact that these are supposed to be key skills in social work practice and yet it often feels as though they are missing. As Paul grew more confident in his own voice, he wanted to get more involved in social work education. He knew the requirements of the

Professional Capabilities Framework inside out! He read all my books and often instigated conversations about social work theory – he had a particular interest in the concept of professional curiosity and reflection, and I see that interest lived out in the use of puzzle pieces and question marks in his art.

Question marks: In many ways the messages of the question marks might be similar to the puzzle pieces and understanding the 'puzzlement' of children. In my work with student social workers, I always encourage them to ask three basic questions of themselves in any situation. What? Why? How? The most important of these (and yet the one that is often missed or skipped over) is *why?* Paul and I always talked about the importance of why. He told me that every child who is looked after wants to know why they are in care, but Paul felt that very few social workers have the courage to support children in exploring the answer to this question. Social workers should ask 'why?' more and help other people to find their why.

Hands: We have laughed about the fact that hands are so hard to draw, but Paul really wanted to use them in his art. He wasn't happy with some of his early 'hands work' and so experimented with using gloves which he filled with plaster. I had visions of the mess as he did it, although it always looked very neat and tidy in the photos he sent! Paul worked a lot on getting the hands right. They were important to him. To me the hand images are all about what is and isn't in our hands. What can we do? Professionals often say, "it's out of my hands now." Is it? Is it really?

Hands were crucially important to Paul, and it may be because of other reasons, as the following story shows:

"One child who came to stay with us could barely take their eyes off the floor and had very limited vocabulary, they flinched if I approached them and assumed the foetal position if I moved my hands towards their head. We could only assume that some sort of violence had been experienced as there was very little known regarding the type of abuse, either witnessed or experienced by them. At night-time this child slept rigid, stiff like a board, unable to relax as if they were preparing themselves for some sort of altercation! For the next three months, I spent a lot of time on my knees in order to effectively reduce my height and be on their level. I established 'walking' routines, where we explored the village we lived in, keeping the same routes, talking about the same things, before introducing new interests. The aim, of course, was to create a safe routine that they understood and could learn to relax in. One day about three months in, the child asked if they could have a hug on my lap. Of course, I obliged, and they sat upright unsure what to do. They asked if they could have a nice hug (they had noticed that we, as a family hug each other, and our other

children often used the phrase 'that was a nice hug'). They leaned into me and for 45 minutes we sat like this. (I was desperate for a wee and had decided that if the worse comes to the worse I'd have to wet myself, as this child needed this hug.) Throughout this time, they stroked my hands and eventually said to me "Babu (their name for me), your hands soft". "Not all men have soft hands, I like soft hands". These words meant so much to me and I cried later on, to hear this little child find words to say he felt safe and knowing that they understood that not all men will hurt them was a real game changer. The real change in this child was seeing their development and understanding of the world accelerate. Using picture cards, we were able to play and talk about what we thought was happening in the picture, what someone might be feeling etc. Their ability to name feelings increased as did their level of empathy and we were fortunate to see the 'waking' of the child they were meant to be. I still get to see this little person (well not so little now). They love stroking my head, face and hands and still tell me I've got soft hands...How good is that! "

I really have no idea which piece of art Paul would have chosen for the cover of this book. He told me that he had something in his mind's eye and that he would create it when he saw the final book pulled together. I selected two pieces of art which show hands for the cover. To me this is something of what they represent:

The first picture is a lone hand. It contains a range of words / labels that were handed to Paul in his childhood. He had no choice. The second image is a pair of hands which holds positive words. The hands are positioned in what some people may see as prayer, reflecting the links to the religious institutions of Paul's childhood. The second image also shows that Paul held many people in his hands with his gentle positive approach. To me, these pictures illustrate some of Paul's story and his journey. The colours on the second image are evocative of a rainbow which is another reason I chose the images.

Religion: Paul spent his childhood in religious institutions. We discussed fears around austerity and the way that the support provided to many children and their families is again coming from religious organisations rather than the state. The way that this might unfold concerned Paul. So called Christian values had not permeated his experiences. The use of Blue as a background on many of his pieces reflects the use of the same shade in much Christian iconography. The development of the 'Coat of Many Colours' into the 'Crucification of Me' (see page 84) shows the way in which Paul's work was developing as a message about religious provision of care. Very recently Paul had started to explore his roots and the Muslim faith which he had been stripped of. This was really important to him. The tributes from Abyd Quinn-Aziz (see page 26) and particularly from Shadim Hussein (see pages 26 - 28) show the fact that Paul was connecting with his faith and his art started to explore this too.

Race / ethnicity: Paul was stripped of his faith and his name by the nuns. This is why I struggled to know how to refer to my dear friend in this book. I feel that I should use Yusuf, but then Paul always called himself Paul to me, and I want to remain faithful to our relationship. Paul's art provides a powerful exploration of his dual heritage. 'White Boy' (see page 94) is such a strong piece and I know that this has spoken to many people. Race is a key theme in Paul's art, and I found talking to Paul about issues like the murder of George Floyd helped me to further connect some of the themes in his work. For example, silence is a recurring theme in Paul's work, and we know that white silence kills. Some of Paul's final artwork reflected the racism that has been endemic in British society for so many years. The words that Rosie had never heard (see page 11) relate to race and racism. Paul's work gives us hugely important messages about the importance of anti-racism in social work.

Masks: Masks appear in Paul's art regularly. Over his lifetime he said that there were so many masks that had been given to him. He felt forced to wear different masks as a child. As an adult he decided to swap the masks for hats! He always described himself as a wearer of many hats. He had shed the masks.

One of the most powerful pieces of art that Paul created was 'Silenced.' Unfortunately, I don't have a good photo of this in exhibition, but I have included sections of the photos that Paul sent to me (see pages 176 and 189). It was such an imposing and quite frankly terrifying piece of art to witness. It is one of the few pieces that Paul titled with confidence. Called 'Silenced' to show how children had been silenced for many years and to reflect what we were beginning to learn about deaths of large numbers of children in religious institutions, it was hard not to be silenced into reflection when you stood in front of this installation art.

Hope: Paul's childhood was brutal, but he held on to the importance of hope. I would go as far as to say that the emerging theme in most of our conversations was hope. I had always felt that hope is a fundamental part of social work, and yet when I had my stroke the social worker who assessed me for discharge said *"You need to come to terms with what has happened to you. It will take time, but you will begin to realise that you will never return to work and will always need support."* They stripped me of every sense of hope. A social worker did that! Social work is about hope. Where has that focus gone?

Paul's view was that the only thing a child is born with is hope. How that child is cared for will either increase or decrease their sense of hope. We would always end our exchanges with hope. It was important to us. In this way Paul became a part of my own healing process, helping me to talk about the impact of my stroke and shed the shame, I wonder if hope is the best antidote to shame?

When Paul died, his hope didn't. This book is all about hope. Essentially it is a journey of hope. That child who stood on my doorstep grew rapidly into a giant of a man. In 1675 Isaac Newton wrote to his fellow scientist Robert Hooke, "*If I have seen further, it is by standing on the shoulders of giants.*" I have seen so much further because of my relationship with Paul. I was privileged to stand on his shoulders.

Paul wanted his work to be used as a learning tool. I hope that what I have written on pages 190 - 193 will help university lecturers, practice educators and students to use Paul's work to learn. If you want to see further, then I advise you to stand on Paul's shoulders.

Over the years I worked with Paul, I learnt a great deal about supporting people to write about and express their own traumatic experiences but as Paul's work became ready for sole publication, I felt that I had become too close to him to do final editing. I was also aware that an independent editor may not be sensitive to Paul's experiences and the importance of his words. After we talked about this, we agreed that I would ask my oldest friend to help support Paul with the final stages of refining his work and I am grateful for the way that Joanne supported Paul to complete the anthology of his poems. I am also very grateful for the way that she supported me to complete the book after Paul's death. As it neared completion, I felt that I had to be honest with Paul that his book might be better published by a large publishing house. I suggested that his work was so good now that it deserved a wider audience than a small independent social work publisher and I advised how he might get a literary agent. He was adamant that his book would never be published by anyone else. I'm still not sure that was the right decision, but it was Paul's and gives the measure of the man. I have tried hard to bring this book to life just as Paul wanted it. We had talked about layout, structure and even font choices but we hadn't agreed on the cover. Not all of the art had been completed and where there is no art for a poem, we have instead included a photograph. For example, the poem 'The Expert on Floors and Halls' is accompanied by a photograph of the floor and hall of Paul's home. Thank you to Joanne who took the photographs along with many of the photographs of Paul's art.

Paul had chosen the title of the book right at the start of the process. I am not sure that it would have been my choice of title, but I have tried to do everything that Paul wanted. I have looked at every message we had; I have gone back over every cake fuelled discussion. I have cried. A lot. I hope that what I have done is what Paul wanted. I hope he is as proud of this book as I am of him. I hope. I always hope.

Tributes to the Author

Paul Yusuf McCormack enriched the lives of many people, some of whom have written something to be included in this book. Reading the messages will give you a sense of the man Paul was and something more of his story.

Paul's family

I am so pleased to be able to help fulfil my husband's ambition and vision of this book. He began to write years after leaving care and I like to think that it was a result of finally being comfortable, safe and happy with his life. He chose 52 poems as it reflected the age at which he began to write. The words poured out of him, as did the tears and rage towards his antagonists. The art expressed these same feelings, and he had the idea to combine the paint with the words. The pain and suffering, along with the frustration and hopelessness of his childhood situation, explodes throughout these pages and I hope it unsettles the people who knew but did nothing.

With one hand I dedicate this book to his lovely children, Kate, Oliver, Michael, Jacob and Aram, of whom he was equally proud and besotted. With the other hand, I dedicate this book to his band of brothers, known as the 'Um Kids, with whom his bond will never be broken.
(Sarah)

My dad was a brilliant man. Brilliant in every single way. And what made him even more so, was that this kind, humble, immensely talented, giant of a man didn't even know how truly brilliant he was. You, on the other hand, would know within seconds, that you were in the presence of someone special.

To look at him, you wouldn't have known that behind that goofy smile and gentle voice lay the absolute horrors and abuse he was subjected to throughout his childhood in the care system. Such memories could have haunted and silenced someone forever, but through art & poetry, my dad found a way to go back to his childhood, to take control and to fight to prevent other children from suffering. He found his voice - a voice you'll hear through each piece in this collection.

It is so heart-breaking that he could not be here today to bask in his achievements (although he was never very good at accepting praise or compliments!) - he had so much more to share with the world and so much more talent to unlock.

I am so proud of every word, every paint stroke and every part of my dad that is entwined and bound within this book. Every page sparks a range of emotions, will draw out meaningful & insightful conversations and will leave you, the viewers of his masterpieces, completely changed.

Dad - Forever in awe of your greatness, forever loved and forever missed.
(Kate)

I am immensely proud of everything Dad has achieved...he didn't have the best of starts...but he didn't let it define him as a person...he let it shape him... let him be a better person...and let him be able to make a difference...he touched the lives of so many...not one person had a bad word to say about him...it just saddens us that he is not here to see the achievements flourish!

We will continue in his footsteps...and make his voice heard!
Love and miss you always Dad!
(Oliver)

There aren't enough words to articulate the greatness that was my Dad, kind, funny, gentle, talented, creative - the list is endless and I'm so proud of everything he achieved in his life.

It's tragic that he's not here today to be able to see this collection come together. The art and words contained in this book are raw, powerful, and emotional, and I'm so proud that after everything he experienced in the early years of his life that he not only found his but gave a voice to many people who couldn't find the courage to speak up.

He was a great inspiration, not only to me, but to everybody lucky enough to have known him, always there to help, encourage and support anybody who needed it, always knowing exactly what to say in the moment.

I'm truly honoured to be able to call him my Dad.
(Michael)

I am so happy and proud for what my Dad has achieved and I'm even more so happy that his legacy will live on forever in his books, poems and artwork. He will forever be in my heart, and he will never be forgotten. Love you Dad and I miss you.
(Jacob)

I feel so happy that Dad brought me in to his life and how lucky I feel to have him for my Dad. He took time to find out about my Kurdish culture and taught me some Kurdish words and how to write my name in Kurdish. I miss him all the time.
(Aram)

The 'Um kids

'Nellie' as I fondly referred to him was one of my dearest friends and my best friend growing up in Father Hudson's Home. He must have been 4 years old when we first met, but we quickly had a bond and looked out for one another. We were brought up in the Cottage homes. Everybody knows that was where the best boys came from, we were smart, intelligent, handsome and great footballers. In our formative years we shared a bedroom, this only made our bond even stronger.

Nellie was a special friend, not just to me but to all the other boys, the 'Um Kids' as we were called. Like us all, Paul suffered in silence growing up in a regime that lacked the parental love and support we all deserved. Paul never moaned or sulked about our predicament, instead he worked hard forging great relationships with his Um Kid family and excelled at school, securing himself a decent job with prospects (this being a very rare occurrence).

As we became the older boys, we became the younger boys' minders and sought to put a stop to a lot of the in-house negative behaviours. As Paul got older, he became very driven to change things, having a louder voice and advocating for those who were unable to or were just frightened.

On leaving the children's home, Paul remained in contact with a lot of the boys, arranging reunions and get togethers. Setting up a Facebook group dedicated to allowing individuals to remain in contact with one another, keeping the 'Um Kid' family together. A lot of boys, me included, often talked about what we would like to do to help others, Paul just got on with it and made it happen. He would spend endless hours phoning and emailing individuals, knowing some of us had very little in our lives. He always remembered birthdays, prompting greetings from all. He never judged, he did not bear any ill will, he just wanted to ease the burden and the hardship we all faced making us all emotionally and socially better equipped.

Paul became a voice and advocate, using his power as an artist to get his point across in his illustrations and poems. He did this all with a heavy heart, opening a pathway for people to see and understand that systematic abuse, hostility, hatred and racism is never ok, and the system should have protected us rather than failing the majority.

Paul was a great talker, he wanted to understand why organisations got it so wrong, reflecting on his own experiences, regardless of the pain he endured reminiscing these difficult times and how vulnerable he allowed himself to be. His goal was always to make things better for us all, educating organisations on the mistakes made but also being adept and showing insight on how to overcome these issues, ensuring the next generation do not suffer as we had.

Paul's sad passing came at a very difficult time for me as only a month earlier my partner had died from a Covid related illness. Both sudden losses were a great shock to me personally and I am not so sure I was in the right frame of mind to deal with these tragedies. I hope I was a good friend and supportive to his loved ones as he was too me.

My thoughts and prayers will always be with you 'Nellie.'
(John [and Michael] Ruggieri)

I knew Paul all of his life because we were raised in the same criminally abusive Roman Catholic Children's Home during the 1960's-1970's. Traumatic as childhood was for Paul, he stubbornly chose hope and identity – not easy for a small boy surrounded by daily terror and neglect. An added heartache for him was the shocking racism which he endured on account of his mixed heritage, at a time when this was a relative rarity in the UK. Yet throughout, he clung onto his sense of self, refusing to be cancelled. When adulthood arrived, he began to heal his broken heart, supremely through his beloved family but also in the astonishing body of artistic work which he left behind as his legacy. And what of his art? It is testimony to the triumph over his crushed spirit; for in his art, he expels the spirit of shame which blighted his childhood. The bright strokes, bold concepts and striking images reflect that inner determination. And yet the power of Paul's art lies in the liminal space between pain and healing. His art is raw yet full of hope. On the one hand, he openly reflects past trauma, almost as if he is re-living it albeit from the safety of adulthood. This is indeed painful for us because his wounds are obvious. And yet, his art penetrates past our inner defences to the deepest parts where we have our being, like the downward flow of water as it finds the lowest point. His art holds a mirror to our own inner insecurities and fears whilst offering the hope of life. So, as you enjoy the art in this book, be prepared to be taken on a journey of self-discovery. For myself, I will always remain inspired by Paul's art, and I am glad this book has been published. Put simply, its contents are the skilful crafting of a true artist who filled his trauma with heaven's gold in the service of others - and that now includes you. Read on.
(Greg Hartigan)

I don't quite know what to say here. I grew up in the children's home under the watchful eye of Paul, who was a little older than me. Paul was the only person who knew how to translate my thoughts and feelings into words, whenever I needed to get them across. He instinctively knew what I needed to say. My words just wouldn't be able to do him justice. It's hard to believe that I won't speak to him again.
(Andy Brookes)

I grew up with Paul from the age of 3 months. Both our mothers are Irish and gave birth to us a month apart in a mother and baby home in Knowle Birmingham. We grew up in the same nursery in Macclesfield called Palotti Hall, and then at the age of 5, I was moved to Father Hudson's, a home for boys in Coleshill, Birmingham. Paul was also placed here. I lost contact with Paul at the age of 14 and we reconnected again around 30 years later.

Meeting up with Paul again after so many years was amazing. His maturity and insight was inspiring. Paul was able to support us in our fostering journey with such honesty. He also helped me to understand and learn about how to deal with rejection, and other difficult emotions and how to support the children in our care.

After our visits to Paul and Sarah's we came home inspired by Paul, that although Paul came from difficult beginnings himself, he harnessed all of his own personal hardships to improve and change the life chances of children in care.

Thankyou Paul, your pain was not in vain.
Miss you.
(Martin, Pauleen and Oliver Hanley)

I remember Paul when I was as young as two years old living in a nursery at Palotti Hall, Manchester. He was 'one of us' (later, known as 'An 'um kid' or to use the vernacular: A homes boy). We grew up along parallel lines but never together. He was in Sister Benahilda's room, I was in Sister Rosemary's room at Palotti. We were so happy there until we were moved to Coleshill aged 5 or 6. Again we were in different houses.

The next thing that I remember about Paul was when we were about 7 or 8 and in an art class at St Anne's school, Chelmsley Wood. Paul showed me how to draw and colour in birds - he was particularly good at it and my favourite of his at the time was a lapwing.

In secondary school Paul was in a different year to me but we became friends in our teens walking to the bus stop together for school and nights saw him sneaking across the grounds with John to watch midweek European football in our house.

In the late 1970's/ early 80's We went to a few Birmingham City games together for the crack and had great fun in our later teens.

I lost touch with Paul until about 2010 and realised how much all of our lives as 'um kids' had changed by then. Paul impressed me as a great connector of people. He went to great lengths to set up get-togethers. He often spoke about rejecting religion in favour of a kindness approach. This sentiment should resonate with all of us because it's all that matters really.

This talented and creative man in art, poetry, delivery of words and love of music who loved to help people and loved to show kindness to others has touched so many lives, not least those of carers and in care.

What a legacy!!!
Thank you Paul, brother. You will always be missed and never forgotten
(Michael Toner)

Wider Care Family

Marks of an Unwanted Rainbow is a book like no other, penned by a giant of a man both in stature and depth of soul. A cherished friend, a man of superb skill and impeccable integrity, a trusted confidant, a man of courage, who through the very essence of his being, reports his world to us through words that find their way through your exterior and into your being. Words that provide vivid, often painful yet truthful insights into the world as he experienced it. Within this honest, vulnerable, and powerful tapestry of thoughts, feelings and emotions are weaved the threads of hope, the hope that Yusuf/ Paul always managed to hold on to. It was this hope that bought me and Yusuf / Paul together, shared threads, connecting us with each other, uniting us both with Your Life Your Story and in our passion, drive and determination to #BeTheDifference in developing our organisation Artifacts. Through our connectivity, shared hope, creativity and understanding we nurtured recognition that we can heal, develop our insights, and grow together, bridging the gaps, crossing the divides, if we remain curious, connect with each other, and are not afraid to explore the tricky stuff, analyse, reflect, get beneath the layers, and encourage others to ask the question why?... And then consider and commit to what we can all do to be the difference…

The work that we began together will continue, Artifacts will become all that we imagined it will be 'no longer marked by an unwanted rainbow' the colour of Yusuf/Pauls soul, his creativity, his courage will continue. His legacy of hope, kindness, compassion, his mark on the world…a very much treasured rainbow.
(Saira-Jayne)

Yusuf was one in a million, one in over one hundred and sixty-six thousand and still rising.

Our first meeting was at the first *Your Life Your Story* weekend in 2017. We spoke of how weird it was that the special weekend was held in a place that was once a children's home. I silently prayed that the children there had not gone through what we had. And at the end of the weekend, when we said our goodbyes that we knew were really hellos; Yusuf asked if he could send me some of his poetry. I wondered just for a moment, if it was a bit like how boys used to make up a tape of their favourite music, a sort of musical message and hand it to you with a certain look in their eye. Little did I know then how much Yusuf loved his wife.

Yusuf sent me reams of poetry to read, he had been busy over the years and had cried for days while processing the pain and hurt from his oh so sad childhood. I cried too - reading his words. I hoped one day I would be able to hold Yusuf's precious words in my hands. Two weeks before he left us, Yusuf had finally completed his collection of poetry. So unfair. I can't wait to hold that compilation in my hands and read his artistry.

A week after the awful news of Yusuf's passing, I was looking at the special painting he gave me. How I cried at the unexpected gift - another 'Rosie moment' as Yusuf called them. He had been saying ever since we first met that he had an image of me in his mind, a small child sat on a huge chair in a library lost in her world of orphan tales. He said that one day he would paint it and he did. When he gave it to me, I hugged him. How I miss those hugs. Yusuf was a good hugger. And in those moments, I felt our pasts, presents, and futures entwine.

Yusuf reminded everyone that he was their brother, we were part of a larger care family. It wasn't even a choice, the connection just was, you can't make it up or pretend, it's too strong. United in our hurt and absolute zest for life and art.

There will be such a huge gap in my life and others collective lives too. How did that happen? One minute Yusuf was here, and the next 'puff' gone, into legend, myth and fairy tale – one of my favourite people disappeared. The gentle giant with the huge heart and capacity for love. I took Yusuf for granted. I let my guard down. I forgot that life is unpredictable. I forgot the lessons of my childhood. I relaxed, stood down. Which is what you do with friends and family and Yusuf was both. I enjoyed Yusuf, the lessons I learnt from him, the healing I had because of him. The fun! I love Yusuf and will miss him. Goodbye dear friend until we meet again. I know Yusuf will be there waiting for when I leave this world too. At last, someone on the other side I want to see again; I'm looking forward to meeting him in that art studio in the sky, one day. The only bit of comfort from his passing.

Until then, dear brother, adieu.
(Rosie)

Colleagues

I was fortunate to meet Yusuf McCormack when he came to help the Cardiff University MA Social Work programme celebrate World Social Work Day in 2018. Almost 100 social work students, academics, practice educators and people who use services were enthralled hearing one his poems and seeing and hearing about his coat of many labels. The messages provided a strong insight into the power of the messages we give children and young people in our care and the weight of the negative labels we burden them with. Yusuf said that *'was good to hear people say they are proud to be a social worker. Sometimes people want to duck and hide about it'*. Much of this resonated with my experience working in children's homes and then later as a social worker, but also the effect of being labelled and having to accept being misnamed. He was a kind man who worked to improve the lives of young people and used his experience to help others develop their understanding and practice. We stayed in touch after this, and I was honoured that he called me brother.

Later, Yusuf wrote an article for the Social Work during Covid magazine and in it, asked us to think through the positive learning we had through the pandemic and the lockdown. He highlighted that the child's welfare must remain paramount in all that we do, and that is what he worked towards in his adult life. Our final edition published following his death paid tribute to him, *'Finally, we would like to pay our respects alongside the many other heartfelt tributes that have been given, to one of the contributors to SW2020 who tragically died from Covid-19 in January this year: the amazing, care experienced activist, artist, father, foster carer, and partner who was Yusuf McCormack. Rest in Power Yusuf. You will always be the difference, and we must continue to learn from the lessons you left us'*.
(Abyd Quinn-Aziz)

It was such a pleasure and a privilege to co-teach with Yusuf at Coventry University. When he entered the room he had so much to give and he would take us on a journey of discovery. I miss him so much but always think of him when teaching these sessions now. His passion and enthusiasm was infectious. On the last occasion, he gave me a copy of a book he co-produced with Siobhan Maclean and Annie. He wrote a personal message inside the cover. When I look at it, I am right back in the lecture theatre with him. Thank you Yusuf for giving so much of yourself to us all."
(Nushra Mansuri)

I first met Yusuf in April 2019 on Twitter, and quickly became intrigued with his life story. Yusuf, ethnically Persian, had grown up in care in the 1960's, and had his name changed to Paul McCormack by social workers so they would have a better chance of finding a family to look after him. Yusuf described his experiences in care to me as traumatic and damaging to his sense of identity. He felt that he'd been stripped of something so precious and grew up feeling a huge sense of loss.

As he grew out of the care system, he began to carve a life out on his own terms. He got married, had his own children, became a foster carer and an adopter. Yusuf was a staunch campaigner for care experienced people and provided training to sector professionals. He was a supremely talented artist and used his pain to fuel his artistry. He was on a journey to understand his own story and identity and found his original birth certificate and discovered his real name was Yusuf. He adopted his birth name and became the Yusuf Paul McCormack we all knew and loved.

A great memory I have of him is when My Foster Family had a talk in London and he came to share his own story. He displayed some of his artwork which included a jacket he had made himself with tags on. Each tag had a derogatory word on it - words he had been called by social workers, foster carers, staff in residential care homes (the people who were entrusted to look after him) and other children in care with him. When he began sharing his story on the stage, the whole room fell silent. Yusuf's story was so captivating, and he shared it with so much conviction, that you couldn't help but listen. This was the type of man Yusuf was.

During our first encounters on Twitter, I was in the early stages of figuring out My Foster Family. My aim had always been to recruit foster carers from diverse communities. I wanted to help children, give them a voice and give them the best experience that would align with their ethnic backgrounds and religions. Meeting Yusuf really honed into me that I was on the right path. We both agreed that not enough consideration went into exploring a child's personal identity and faith when they were placed in the care system. Much like Yusuf, in the 70's and 80's children were stripped of their sense of self and moulded into amiable robots to be placed anywhere that'll take them. While much has changed, Yusuf and I discussed in detail how much more the sector needed to change, and how we would go about working towards that change.

During the time I was lucky enough to know Yusuf, he would join me during my events for My Foster Family, sharing his story around the country. We spent hours talking about our life experiences and changes we'd like to see in the sector on our long drives to different events. In Islam, it says you don't know someone until you've travelled with them or done business with them. On one occasion, I drove from Bradford to Birmingham to pick up Yusuf and we drove to London with our other friend, Magribi. I remember the journey vividly because we all had our own unique take on life, and we talked for hours. We ended up in Regents Park Mosque and myself and Magribi went to pray. We had missed the prayer time, but there were a small number of men praying in a line and we quickly joined them. Yusuf sat in the corner and watched us. When we had finished our prayers and went our own separate ways, Yusuf said to me he was amazed at the sense of brotherhood he had just seen. He explained to me he felt he'd been witness to something quite special, seeing strangers come together to pray and being in the mosque he felt a sense of belonging. No words needed, just understanding. This is an indication of the profound sense of loss Yusuf felt due to his years in care and his identity being stripped of him.

In our private chats Yusuf would talk to me about his family and the special efforts they make as a team to look after each other and all the children that came into their lives, he had so much love and pride for his family. I always felt his home must have been a special place.

Yusuf often told me the way children were handled in care could be done so much better. Over the years, he connected with other people who had also been in care in the hopes of creating a movement so big, change would have to follow in the sector. He saw a future where children wouldn't have to give up their culture and faith to be accepted into a home. Understanding these differences and dealing with them accordingly wouldn't cost the state any money, but it would mean treating children in care with respect and dignity and achieving better outcomes when children eventually leave care.

On 8th January 2021 Yusef was going to join me for a zoom meeting I had organised and he sent me the following message

"Salaams Shadim, I had thought I'd be available for this evening. Unfortunately I'm unwell with a throat and chest infection. Inshallah it's not Covid-19 as I don't appear to have those symptoms but it's still a bit worrying. Hopefully I'll be feeling much better real soon, but it has knocked some of the stuffing out of me. I'm sure this evening will be a success, a lot of passionate people are getting involved which gladdens my heart. Take care for now Shadim bhai & inshallah we'll speak soon."

I replied insha'Allah (God willing). Will be plenty more look after yourself pal.

A few days after our chat, I heard the sad news that Yusuf had left this world. I informed everyone who knew him and we all shared a prayer for Yusuf.

Yusuf was not only a friend to me, but a brother in faith and a trusted advisor. He joined the advisory board at My Foster Family and was always readily available for me to bounce ideas off. In the short time we knew each other, he made an impact on my life in a profound way, and I'll continue to honour his memory and wishes through my work.

(Shadim Hussein)

Social Work Students

I 'met' Yusuf virtually when he was introduced to the Social Work Student Connect Team by Siobhan. As a relative newcomer to the world of the care experienced, his art, poems and views have left a lasting legacy with me that I will carry through my career. I work with older adults and until that time, I'd never really considered how their childhood experiences might manifest in later life. Yusuf helped me see the crucial importance of understanding how a person has come to the later stages of their life. Now, the first thing I want to know about people is their life story so that I can try to understand their perspective better. I pass this as a message to all my colleagues and current students to help them to also understand the 'Why?' for people. The difference it has made to my practice is immense. Paul's mantra to 'Be the Difference' is at the heart of all I do. I treasure Yusuf's artwork which sits behind me when I work at home as a visual reminder of why we do what we do. Thank you, Yusuf, for your insight and ethos. I will hold it close.
(Chris Norman, Social Work Student Connect)

I only knew this giant of a man for a very small amount of time, but he certainly made an impact on me. When I first met him at a webinar his smile lit up the 'zoom' room and the silence amongst the virtual audience was tangible as you could tell everyone was absolutely transfixed by Yusuf's story.

I have some of Yusuf's art. I framed one piece and it kept me company as I finished my final year during the pandemic and I now carry around the other, a small label, in a little pocket within my work rucksack as I venture out into my newly qualified role. It reminds me to 'Be the Difference.'
(Becky Salter, newly qualified social worker)

I only knew Yusuf for a brief time, yet as a care experienced social work student, he felt like a friend from the moment we first spoke at the care experienced conference. We met just that one time and spoke several times in brief over social media, the man was a force of peace, everything about him radiated reflection, calm and kindness. I've heard Yusuf described as a gentle giant, but this doesn't come close to the feeling of calm that he gave to others. It was an honour.
(David Grimm)

A fortunate reply to a message on twitter led to my involvement with a webinar project and meeting Yusuf. He willingly gave his time to discuss his early and current life experiences, I didn't know it at the time, but I really needed to hear what he said! My journey has taken a few twists and turns and my wife and I now care for a little girl on a full-time permanent basis. I have taken so much from Yusuf's work around the importance of identity and love and I am so grateful for him for sharing.
(Kelly Bentley-Simon)

Joanne Roebuck who helped to edit this book

When I was first asked to help Paul refine his poems for this book, I had no idea of the journey it would take me on. My first surprise, as someone with no experience of social care, then or now, was the brutality of the experiences Paul had endured. I was horrified that so-called responsible adults could be so cruel to innocent children.

My second surprise after speaking to Paul on the phone, and later meeting him in person, was how such a gentle, caring, sensitive and lovable man could have emerged from those dreadful experiences. This is a phenomenon which continues to amaze me but, after the shock of Paul's untimely demise, also deeply saddens me. This book would have been a physical manifestation of his healing, healing which only began to blossom a relatively short time ago. It feels to me such a great tragedy that he only experienced a few years of life beyond the moment when he 'let it all go'.

The third surprise of my involvement with Paul was how much commonality there was between us, particularly in the way our individual pasts had shaped us. I had not suffered the same upbringing as Paul, but I had experienced abuse and, as we talked openly to one another, we began to learn more about ourselves and the way the threads of our respective childhoods had stitched together to make us who we are. This increased understanding was something we both relished in our thirst for greater self-awareness and healing.

For children who have experienced less love than they deserved and more hurt than they ought, healing is an ongoing process as it is difficult to completely escape from the shadows of the past. However, if we're lucky enough, we have new experiences and encounters which move us further along in our healing journey. Meeting Paul was such an encounter for me, and I very much hope that his book will move others in the right direction on their journeys. Even though he's no longer here in person, and I will forever be sad that our blossoming friendship was terminated too soon, his words will continue to be an inspiration to me. He was a phoenix that rose magnificently from the ashes of his past, and he used all that he had learnt in his 'former' life to help others. It is my heartfelt wish that he can continue to do this through the creativity of the latter years of his life, which have made their way onto the pages of this publication through the love, kindness and dedication of his wife, Sarah, and his colleague and great friend, Siobhan.

(Joanne)

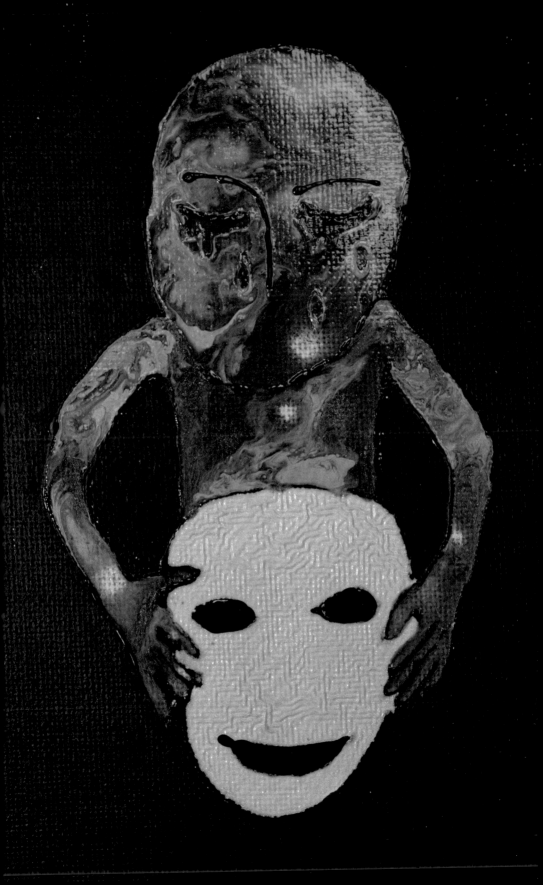

My Voice, Our Voice

One day I'll get my say,
I'll find my strength,
My courage,
The courage that's kept me going.
I'll tell you my story.
Maybe then you'll hear the pain,
Maybe then you'll see the torment,
Maybe then you'll listen to my anguish.

Or maybe you'll cover your ears,
And close your eyes,
Hoping I'll go away.
But I won't!
I'm here,
I'm alive,
I survived.

My story isn't only mine.
It's just one voice,
A speaker for those
Who are still scared,
Still ashamed,
Still afraid of not being believed,
Of waking their demons,
Of the anxiety, torment
And lack of sleep
That will follow when
They let their nightmares loose.

I stand here,
Emotionally stripped,
Vulnerable,
All my protective veneer gone,
Telling you my story,
So that I and others can sleep,
Sleep without fear.

My Story

A deep breath vacates my chest,
Its sigh joins the atmosphere,
And my chest stirs with relief.

Heaving, I steady myself.
I swallow, then pause.

Finally, I will tell you my story.
It isn't pretty,
Unpleasant is more fitting,
But it's my story.

Its relevance in shaping me isn't lost,
But it doesn't have to define me.

It tells you how it splintered me,
Fractured and cracked me.

My inner self trickled
Through the seams of a broken body.
My emotional me evaporated from my
heart,
And mingled with the ether
To be blown away with the wind.

Tinged with sadness, hurt and fear,
Occasionally hope surfaces,
But only occasionally.

I will tell you how they
Tried to smash me,
Purging every part of me,
Physically, soulfully, emotionally.

But somehow, they failed
To completely break me,
Though they came so close.

Was this my fate?
All of us here,
Subjected to untold violence,
Violence of word,

Violence of deed,
Violence in all its disguises
Visiting us repeatedly,
Like the ebb and flow of waves
Beating against the rock edge.
Eventually sand will be all that
remains.

Sometimes I was so beaten,
So battered, so emotionally vacant,
That the mercy of death
Would have been a comfort.

Now, something stirs,
Breaching the surface of me:
Anger, fight, justice
All claw their way
From inside my mind.

An insurgence of belief in me grows
strong,
A beat pulsating through my veins,
Flowing faster, gaining power.

I'm shaking, shaking,
Trembling, as words leave my mouth.
My mind explodes,
Desperate to rid itself
Of the pain it has held for so long.

Words spill forward,
Gaining speed,
Gaining confidence,
Free at last,
Given a voice,
A vehicle to shout,
To tell those that refused to listen,
To speak for those who still cannot.

And breathe,
Breathe,
Let go.

The Creation of Me

Her eyes glance to the side,
They visibly sparkle.
Eyebrows raised,
His teeth slowly appear,
And his mouth broadens into a smile.

Her cheeks flush,
The heat rises within her.
She turns away,
Looking downwards.
Momentarily she gasps.

Her heartbeat can surely be heard,
As it booms out its intent.
She wills it to be quiet,
As her chest heaves,
Her hands entwine,
Fingers twisting,
Squeezing each other,
And she dares to look up.

Enticed by his exotic looks,
His gentle manner (the words my
mother used),
His head, slightly tilted to the left.
His shy smile remains,
Whilst his eyes bury deep into her soul.

Forgotten,
The promise to look after her brothers,
Forgotten,
The ring on her finger,
Engaged to another.
When the cat's away the mouse will
stray!
Forgotten,
Her virtue,
Her sanctity,
Her chastity,
Her belief.

The call of love is far greater,
Or is it purely lust?
Her need to satisfy desires,
Her fantasies,
Her primal urge,
Her primitive needs.
Greed consumes her,
A need she hadn't felt before.
The danger,
The excitement!

Bamboozled by his charm,
His manners,
His ways,
So polite,
And his voice
So velvety,
So soft,
He almost speaks
In a whisper.

Her mind floats off
On the breath of a cloud.
Impeccable standards!
And he kisses her hand.

He dressed so smart,
Shirt, suit and tie.
Creases sharp, crisp,
Defined by their cutting edge.

Hair thick, wavy, with a shy curl
And black, so very black.
His eyes dark brown,
Dark, deep,
With hidden softness.

Oh! And scented golden skin,
Kissed by the sun,
Perfumed by the gods,
To intoxicate her mind,

Scented to infuse dreams.
Rationale has gone, disappeared.
Caution follows hot on its heels,
And flies out the same window.
The fear of being caught
No longer holds her back.
Instead, it excites her.

The need to satisfy herself,
To fulfil her needs,
Takes over.
The spice,
Her greed,
The heat she feels,
All mix together when their lips meet.
Entwined lovers in that moment,
Their urgency fuelled by passion,
Control no longer theirs.
The inevitable
Is their shared goal.

And satisfaction is measured
By the hours of the night.
His breath cools her shoulders
And she listens to his heart singing
Rumi,
Just for her.

Pyusuf

Firstborn

The first sound I ever heard
Was the drum beat of my mother's heart.
It soothed me in her womb with its
rhythmic chant,
It offered me comfort, it offered
reassurance
As I sheltered in the darkness,
Tucked away in the warmth of her body.
It nurtured my well-being,
It became my constant,
It was all I knew.

I was the first to feel her worries,
Her anxieties, her fears, her anger,
Her concerns, her sorrow.
She never hid them from me.
Instead, she spoke in hushed tones
Of being found out,
She spoke in cryptic whispers
Of her terrible 'sin'.
I didn't understand it, I just felt it
As it seeped through my being, feeding
my heart.

Softly spoken, speaking poetically in Gaelic,
She told stories of her past, her
history, her family,
And she spoke of Rumi and ghazals,
Remnants from a father I would never
know.
She spoke my name, the name they
chose together,

But I don't remember it now.
Officials stole it and another was chosen,
A name 'gifted' to me by a regime
So that my differences would not be
recognised,
So that I would live a life unnoticed.
She heard my first cry, and cried with me
When I entered the world.
I screamed, protesting,
Unaware of my chosen path.
I felt her tears, her love and her fear
As she clung onto me,
Her cloak of feelings,
Shrouded around us both.
Was there desperation in her touch
As she clasped onto me through
Donated knitted blankets?
I imagine so.

Her tears spilled slowly when she cried,
Each one kissing my cheeks in silence,
Shining momentarily like spilled glitter.
And we gazed into each other's eyes,
Mine innocently sparkling, quizzical,
Offering hope and new beginnings.
In return, I witnessed the sadness of
her soul,
Reflected through the mirrored windows
of her eyes,
As her tears wetted her face, and
silently fell away.

Six Weeks

Broken promises,
Hidden lies,
That's what they offered you.
They took your babies,
Offering them a chance,
Promising them a home,
Families, good families,
Families who want them,
Families who'll give them
All the things you can't,
Families who'll love them,
And won't even mind
That they're brown!

They never recognised your hurt,
Refused to acknowledge your pain,
And your anguish.
Instead, they gifted you guilt,
Insisting you'd be better off
Without this burden which
Would only hold you back.
Six weeks they gave you,
That's all, six weeks.
Six weeks to torment you,
To embed the guilt
You already felt,
To teach you
The error of your ways.

And you, well,
You got to gaze in wonder
At this precious jewel,
This innocent life
Who looked to you for love,
For hope,
For security;
Infant eyes,
Full of expectation,
Full of desire, of longing,
Full of belief in you.
You held them,
Stroking their cheeks,
With your arms
Wrapped around them,
Whilst you whispered your story

Of how you loved them,
And always would,
How you had no option,
How it's best for them,
A chance of a better life.
But we were unaware.
Safe in the comfort of
Your love,
Your warmth,
We weren't prepared
For what came next.
You couldn't have known,
You wouldn't have let us go,
Would you?

Bonds were formed between us,
And when the time came,
Denying you a mother's need,
Ripping us apart,
You left, head down,
Tears streaming,
Heart breaking,
And, for some,
A blessed relief!
Our primal instincts kicked in,
And we screamed.
Confused, alone,
Fear replacing love,
Uncertainty became our bedfellow.
Our cries were unheard,
Or ignored.
No one came,
You never came.

We didn't know,
We didn't understand.
Passed to institutions,
Our fate was determined,
Our lives mapped out,
Our ethos ingrained
To always be humble,
To always be grateful
For our opportunity in life.

Six weeks is all we had,
Six weeks.

Our Mantra

"Where are ye from?"
"The gutter Sister, the gutter."
We respond in unison with such gusto,
Happy to shout out,
Excited to see her positive reaction.
She wrings her hands,
As a smile creeps across her face.
Her eyes narrow as she looks at each
of us,
"Which of ye are from the gutter?" she
barks.
"Me, Sister, me, Sister!"
Arms waving,
Jostling to be noticed.
Nippers sitting, legs crossed,
Vying to be seen,
Vying to be heard,
Nudging, pushing,
Shoving each other,
So they can take the accolade of being
heard first.
"Whose mother comes from the gutter?"
Almost said with a sneer, there's a hint
of spite.
"Mine Sister, mine Sister, mine Sister!"
The children struggle to remain seated,
So very desperate to be heard,
Smiling at each other joyfully,
Swelling with pride
That **they** were the one acknowledged,

That **they** got the nod from the
shrouded crow in black.
Settling back now, to bask in being
heard,
Grinning from ear to ear,
Whispering, "See! I'm from the gutter."

"Be quiet!" she snarls.
Arms folded she adjusts herself
And straightens her crucifix.
She smirks and spits out,
"And where did she meet your fathers?"
Her finger is pointing, as she gives a
rueful stare.
"The gutter, Sister, the gutter, Sister!"
She's almost reached her crescendo,
She's near her climax.
"And why are ye from the gutter?"
"Me Sister, me Sister!
"We're black bastards, Sister, black
bastards!"
She nods, her eyes looking at each of
our faces.
She utters an 'Ahem',
Now it's her turn to smile
With benevolence.
Sitting back, she swells smugly,
Basking with the satisfaction of our
answers,
Our mantra.

Time to Turn Away Child

Close your eyes little child,
Now's not the time to look up.
Let the weight of your eyelids take over,
Succumb to their heaviness,
Close them tight,
For the world is ugly right now.
Don't hold their stare.

Close your ears little child,
Listening will damage you more.
Don't let the words invade you.
Deflect their venom and hatred,
Don't take them to heart,
'Cos they will only harm you.
They only want to destroy you.

Close your heart little child,
Don't feel anymore.
Become a stone, become a thing.
Violence is yours to suffer,
For you to take alone.
Take it, 'cos soon it will cease,
And you can rest once more.

Close your mind little child,
Don't think too hard.
Understanding is a concept too far.
Now is the time to turn away,
Remove yourself, escape the madness.
'What ifs' can be your dream,
If only for a passing moment.

If you don't see, hear, feel, think,
Then it doesn't have to be real.
Your heartbeat is your constant,
Listen to its song.
It beats for you,
Just for you,
Hold on.

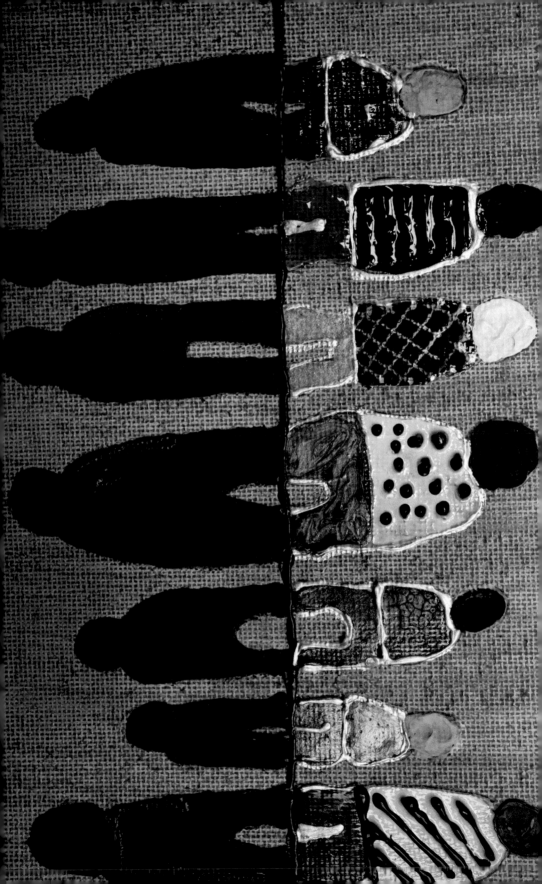

Cake for Tea

I love St Patrick's day, it's great!
The green, the gold, the white!
They said I can be Irish for today,
And we're having cake for tea.

They're all smiling here!

Tricolour flags, harps pinned to jumpers,
A clod of shamrock wedged to our chests.
And the beloved man himself, Saint P.,
In his green frock, surrounded by tinsel.

Wearing a benevolent smile!

His foot squashes a serpent
Reminding of the evil that
Resides in ones so small, like us,
Or so we're told.

No smiles for us then!

Our badges are worn with pride
To celebrate a glorious day,
A feast day,
And we're definitely getting cake for tea!

That makes me smile!

Hair, cut, wetted, combed with distinct
Partings carved into the side of our heads.
Faces cleansed and cleansed again,
Polished by her spit and used hanky...

Wiping the smile from my face!

"You'll not be making a holy show of me
Ye dirty little tramp."
Words of 'comfort' for this auspicious
day,
But it's okay,
'Cos we're definitely having cake for tea.

My smile returns!

Standing straight and tall like soldiers,
Arms by our sides, ready for battle
despite our age.
Sunday 'best' crease-free clothes, shoes
polished,
Gleaming, and socks held up with garters.

No place for smiles!

We await the crow in black with beads
and cross,
Hands and necks presented for inspection.
Tutting, she walks the line, slapping, pinching,
Purposefully pecking, removing smirks
that dare to show,
Gifting an extra 'glow' to cheeks already
shining red,
And extra sparkle to eyes already wet
from tears.
But it's ok,
'Cos we're definitely having cake for tea.

I smile within!

Our audience awaits, such good people,
Seated in their pews, hymn books gripped,
Ready in anticipation as we joyfully
march in pairs
To the music, 'Hail Glorious St. Patrick'.
So many smiles!

They rise, glancing at us, some pointing.
We can hear their laughter, utterings and
mutterings,
Snide, sly whispers, but loud enough for
us to hear,
"Well, God love 'em, thinking they're Irish.
Would ye look at the poor little sods,
Aww, the poor unfortunate little bastards."

But we don't care
'Cos today...
We're definitely having cake for tea!

A Trouble Child, a Troubled Boy.

A trouble child, a troubled boy,
A boy always in trouble.
Descriptions, labels,
Worn each day by me,
This troubled boy who feels the words,
The pain, the intent.

So many conversations in my head,
Searching for answers,
Confused and tied up
With religious doctrine.
God has a plan!

'You're here to teach lessons
That need to be learned,
To address the sins
Committed by those
Who should have known better.'

That mantle is a lot to take on at 5!
Innocence instead,
Fuels my expectations,
My acceptance that
This is how it is.

Happiness is always just out of reach,
No matter how hard I stretch.

Small crumbs of comfort
Are favours I devour,
Nurturing them, keeping them safe within,
Marvelling at the warm embrace I feel.
Selfishly hidden away,
They're not for sharing.
They're all I have that's mine,
Regurgitated when required
To show me I matter.

A boy always in trouble!
That's how they see me.

I just see a boy.

Tuck Shop

I love Saturdays,
Pocket money day,
It's bostin'!

Tuck shop.
Yeahhhh!
The rush to line up,
Boys in varying degrees of excitement,
Nudging, shoving,
Poking 'n pushing each other
To get into their place.

Big kids first,
Them is the rules.
Nippers always at the end.
Anticipation is a tingling feeling
From the feet up.

Shh, shh, shh is passed down the line.
The ritual is about to commence.
"Right, are 'yees' ready,"
She crows.
She floats along the line.
Small balls of tumbleweed dust
Collect on the hem of her habit
As she glides to the tuck shop door.
She hovers next to the lined-up children,
Her feet never seen; does she even
have any!

Slowly, purposefully, eyeing us one at a
time,
Our expectant faces follow,
But we don't hold her stare.
Looking downwards is the mark of
respect
That must be shown.
As she passes, necks crane forward,
Turning in unison to the left,
Is she there yet?

Halt.
She stands outside the door, key poised,
Attached to a long wielding chain
Along with the crucifix effigy of our lord.
He died to save others,
He died because of me,
He's used to attack our skulls
And open our ears to the word of God!

Turning the key,
She slyly glances back up the line.
Then, the turn of the handle
And she opens the big red door
To our holy grail,
The chamber we all dream about
That hides our desires and wishes.

I know she's picking up her book.
I see it in my mind's eye.
It's filled with names and numbers,
Our number always before our name,
Our savings too,
And all our deeds!
Will I be lucky this time?

Pressing against each other,
The queue shuffles forward as one,
Like a giant caterpillar.
Our weekly 'tuck-shop shuffle' is in motion.
It's great! It's brilliant!
I can hardly contain myself,
Desperately trying to inhale the sweet
incense.
Tuck shop day is just the 'bestest' ever
feeling.

Thoughts interrupted
As she squawks out,
"There'll be no pushing now!
Whoever's doing it'll get nothing,
Mark my word!"

A chime of,
"It's the nippers Sister!"
Is proffered by the big boys.
It placates her for now.
It's always us that get the blame,
But nothing can change our grinning
faces,
Filled with excitement and expectation.

The first in line is beckoned forward.
Ears straining, I can hear her ask,
"What are ye having?"
'Erms' and pauses
Whilst selections are made.
I imagine fingers pointing
As eyes scan the shelves.
And then the clunk of scales
As weights are added to measure.
A clatter, as sweets spill from the jars
Into the bowl.
What a noise! I love it!
My throat swallows,
I can almost taste their selection.
There's the sound of rustling
As paper bags come alive,
Expanding into shape
As they devour the pouring sweets.

Alert, our smiling faces, eyes alight,
Watch, as the big 'uns'
Emerge with their treasure.
They've got their spoils,
But that's not enough.
Demands with threats are made,
Spat at us in hushed tones.
Extras they want:
You'll get your fucking head kicked in
If you don't agree!
I don't care 'cos it's tuck shop day!

I can nearly see the whole door.
Soon I'll be able to smell the open jars.
I picture each one, the colours, the shapes,
Their names, each type of sweet.
Will she have new ones?
I know 'em all so well,
Engraved on my mind,
Etched in my heart:
Pear drops, lemon drops, bon bons,
Sherbets, flying saucers, fruit salads,
And black jacks of course,
With their picture of 'Golly'!
Their smells creep up the line
To infuse our senses.
Necks craned, noses outstretched,
Pointing upwards and forwards
To inhale this deliciousness.
Mmm, heaven!

My heartbeat increases with expectation.
I can feel the suspense in my chest.
Oooh! Oooh! What to have?
It's so exciting! I'm so excited
My feet are doing their own dance.
The queue is getting smaller.
I hate it that I'm at the end,
But I am the littlest.

My hands worry each other
As I turn them over.
Just one more boy, then it's me.
It's my turn next.
It's nearly my turn.
Please forget, please!
It's my turn now.
I enter the gateway to my heaven
Intoxicated by its aroma,
Senses alert to the multiple smells,
Colours, shapes, sweets,
And her demeanour.
I look at her, but not for long,

She might remember.
I choose quickly and politely,
My little hands behind my back,
Fingers crossed.
I always know what I want.
I hold my breath as she hands me a bag.
It's filled with pear drops, a gobstopper,
And two black jacks.
Mmm, I love pear drops.
"You can have one if you like?"
I offer politely, 'cos that's
What you should do to a Sister.
She's told me enough times,
'Manners maketh the man'.

A smile appears on her face
As she hands me the bag,
But, in an instant, she pulls back.
My fingers are left touching air,
Grasping at nothingness,
Holding on to the pretence,
A pretence that was a bag of sweets!
"Didn't I say you can't have pocket
money,
Didn't I?" she snarls.
I nod and mumble,
"Yes Sister."
"You little sneak! That's what ye are."
"Yes Sister." I manage to whisper.
"You're a sneaky little liar!
Oh, you think you're so smart, don't
you?"
I know better than to reply.
I mumble, "I'm sorry!"
My head has already dropped.
Tears fill my eyes
As I look for an escape route,
But I can't even see my shoes
As I walk to the ominous cane
cupboard
For today's selection,

The only selection I'm having.
Others look on, relieved it's not them.

Zoo Time

They come in their droves,
By the coach load,
To look at us,
Stare at us,
Point at us,
Whilst we eat our tea.

If they're lucky they'll get to
Watch us,
Laugh at us,
Or remind us
How lucky we are,
Whilst we eat our tea.

Some of them will
Speak with us,
Talk at us,
Sympathise with us,
Whilst we eat our tea.

Then return to their coach,
Happy they are giving to us,
Praying for us,
Happy they're not one of us,
Whilst we eat our tea.

Look I Can Dance!

Watching,
I'm always watching,
From the shadows.

The side-lines are my limit now,
Trying to anticipate the direction of
your vision,
Wanting, daring to hope....
Pick me, pick me, I almost scream aloud.

I'll be so good.
Look! I can dance!

The children dance
To strange music only they can hear.
Toddlers, infants,
All jumping, swooshing, spinning, twisting.

But in the shadows it's still.
Eyes alert, watchful, searching.
Still hoping, desperately hoping,
To be the chosen one...
Pick me, pick me!
I'll never give you cause to return me.

I'll be so good.
Look! I can dance!

I'm older now.
I'm still waiting.
The shadows offer me comfort,
A place of solace.

My eyes are glazed,
They look with hope no more.
They know your eyes
Will never meet or hold
Their gaze of expectation.

Your glance is now of pity,
A cursory look.
It searches other faces,
It offers others a chance.
Hope is still theirs.
Pick me, pick me,
Is a ghostly echo now.

I'll be so good.
Look! I can dance!

Another Day...Another Year

Today was another bad day!
I get a lot of these.
People came,
People went.
They took a look through the fences.
They didn't stay long,
They never do.
And I'm still here,
Another day,
A week,
A month,
Another year

Unclaimed,
Not wanted,
Are difficult to assimilate.
Confusion and a furrowed brow
Animate my face,
Unsure what I've done
To still be here,
Another day,
A week,
A month,
Another year

I don't look at them anymore,
There isn't any point.
I don't even warrant a glance these days,
As the 'crow' whispers in their ears
And shakes her head
At any interest shown my way.

So, I'll stay
Another day,
A week,
A month,
Another year

Hope fades,
Evaporating before my eyes,
And I've turned away.
My dreams,
No longer an expectation,
Are distant; they avoid me.
Reality is very clear.
I'm still here, we all are,
Another day,
A week,
A month,
Another year.

I can't let you see
The stains of my tears,
The despair that now shadows my face
And mirrors my heart.
Belonging remains out of reach.
Still, I have my 'brothers' here,
That's something.
But we all wait, unwanted,
Another day,
A week,
A month,
Another year.

Last Collection Time
Monday to Friday

9.00am

A **4.00pm** or later collection is made
from the Postbox at
Hartshorne Church

The latest collection in the area is made
at **6.30pm** from
Burton Delivery Office,
Falcon Close, Burton

Saturday

7.00am

Every Day I Write a Letter.

Every day I write a letter.
I ask you, I plead with you
To come and get me.
I even pray!
I demand you come,
I demand you fetch me
To realise my thoughts,
Fulfil my dreams,
My hopes, desires,
My wishes.

It overwhelms me.
It consumes me.
My head's full
Of so many words,
Wrestling with each other,
Fighting, struggling,
To make sentences
Worthy for you to read.

I know what I want to say,
I think, and yet...
I don't, I'm clueless.

My words are clumsy,
Infantile in their arrangement,
Childlike in their delivery.
I want you to like them.
Please don't be ashamed of me,
That cross is mine to bear.

How do you write to a stranger?
What would they like to hear?
My mental pen, poised to say
something,
Hovers, stutters, stammers
In its attempts to form a word,
Just one word!
Sheets of paper
Strewn across my mind's floor,
Crumpled, discarded,
Crossed out, rejected,
Unworthy for your eyes.
How do you write to a stranger
Who's not a stranger,
Just someone you don't know?

You're Not with the Babies Now

A scream pierces the silence.
The suddenness,
The speed,
The shock.
Her fist connects with my face.
I never saw it coming,
I never saw it coming!

Pain ricochets,
Abject panic ensues.
Eyes wide, I need to escape.
Hurled from the chair,
I instinctively reach upwards
With my hands,
To protect me,
To defend me.

Her fists, at speed,
Continue with their mission.
Confused, dazed, stunned,
My head is throbbing.
Clumps of hair lie on the floor.
Are they mine?

My childhood shattered,
Gone, in an instant!
"You're not with the babies now",
She spits viciously.

Her face is so close to mine
Her words brush against my cheek,
The heat of her breath
Claws its way over my skin,
Her smell infiltrates my nostrils,
And I can taste her.

Her spittle showers the side of my face,
Stinging me with its poisonous venom.
I stare with wide eyes at the floor,
Unable to focus as tears cloud my vision.

Shreds of hair, my hair,
Lie beneath me and on me.

There's a cough in the background,
Or is it a snigger?
Are the others laughing at me?
Jerked forward from my momentary
thought,
She yanks me by my collar,
Shaking me as I writhe in panic
To break free.

"Ye...can....stop...that...sniv...ell..ing!"

Her fist beats out each word,
Each syllable,
To some tune
Only she can hear.
My sleeve is streaked with tears,
Snot, blood,
Like the entrails
Of a recently killed carcass.

I can make out the outlines of others'
faces,
Their eyes not reflecting their smiles.
Concern and fear are hiding there,
Relief that it's not them.
One puts his finger to his mouth,
His eyes hinting a suggestion.
I understand immediately
And cease my protests,
My screams, my struggle.

With one arm she lifts me,
Throwing me into my chair.
I cling on, not daring to look up.

My mashed potato, fish fingers and
peas
Are cold now.
Slowly I chew,
The taste of tears, blood and snot
Accompanying each mouthful.

I'm not with the babies now!

The Boy with the Broken Smile

Snapped laces and scuffed shoes,
Dirty knees, socks at half-mast
Barely cover grubby shins.

Scratches and trickles of blood,
Mingling with engrained dirt,
Paint road maps across his legs.

Ripped short trousers,
Two sizes too big for him,
Held in place with his favourite snake belt,
Buttoned flies neither up nor down.

A shirt that's forgotten its fastened
sequence,
Dangling threads,
The consequence of arguments with a
hedge.

Hands patterned in shades of muddy brown,
Punctuated with blobs of blood, his blood.

His worried away fingernails,
A physical narration of his story,
Attempt to squeeze into his bulging
pockets
Which are filled with stones.

Hair, undecided of the fashion to
follow,
Pointing in all directions, refusing to be
tamed.

Face splattered with a patchwork of
dirt,
And dried-up tear tracks
Smudged beneath his dark eyes
Which squint as he stares vacantly,
His head twisted slightly,
Avoiding the sun's intrusion on his
being.
A broken smile worn on his face
Masks his hurt and hides how he feels.

Night Creeps In

He knew what it meant
To find sleep under the cover of fear.
Night-time is accompanied,
It's never alone.
It searches for him,
Seeking him out,
Touching him
With its cold breath on his back.

Eyes wide open,
Waiting,
Waiting.
If he turns now,
Will he face his demon,
His tormentor?

The daytime offers little relief.
It comes with its own agenda,
Teasing him,
Tormenting him,
Dangling an opening,
An opportunity of escape.
And for a fleeting moment he can
believe
He has the chance to fly.
But the door is shut firmly.

His mind needs to drift now!

They know what's happening,
Yet choose to ignore,
And say their prayers!

He likes the feel and smell
Of an empty church,
Surrounded by statues,
Light streaming through
Stained glass windows,
Lighting up the shadows,
Painting silhouettes on walls.

The scent of incense lingers,
Clinging to the air he breathes,
Enveloping him with its arms,
To comfort him.

He sits in silence,
His mouth slightly open,
Eyes lowered under the heaviness of
his eyelids,
And he watches as the candle's flame
becomes extinguished.

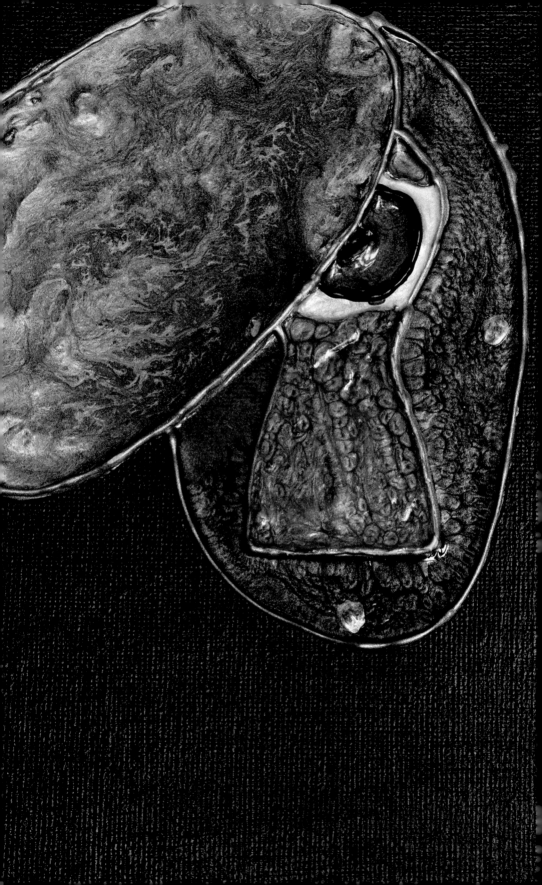

Innocence taken

Don't touch me!
P L E A S E.
I don't want to,
I don't like it.

Rising heat,
Face so hot,
Tears sting my cheeks,
And snot dangles.

I wipe my arm across my face.
Heaving, gasping, gulping for breath.
My sobs engulf my whole body,
Rising, falling.

I flinch, step back
As he comes closer.
NO!
I don't want to.

Gaping, gibbering,
My words struggle to get out,
To make any sense.

Panic has taken over.
My vision is blurred by tears.
I can't escape,
I'm cornered.

Please,
No!
He offers me a smile............

Marks of an Unwanted Rainbow

Small fingers stroke my bruises,
Softly, gently, tracing outlines.
Beguiled, I marvel at their colouration,
Their discolouration,
Distorted complexion,
Tainted pigmentation,
A blended pallet of colour
Caused by blows, kicks,
Fists, sticks,
By you.

My gifted badges of honour to wear,
My stitched-on badges of shame
For others, who look,
To dismiss and ignore.

A hue of black and purple,
Smudges of dusky yellow,
With threads of woven grey,
And sometimes even smears of red and
blue,
With a hint of green.

My tears drop silently inside me,
Unable to wash them away.
Stained like fragments of coloured glass,

A church window to my soul,
But nothing so glorious for me,
My marks of an unwanted rainbow.

And bruises present in many guises,
You have to look past the shades
To see beyond the colours
To the damage that's been done.

The outside layers will recover,
That pain is fleeting, it's only for now.
But the bruises to my heart,
The bruises to my mind,
They shy away, they hide,
They fuel my self-worth,
They determine what I feel,
They contribute to my thoughts,
They paint my nightmares, and yet,
My face will mask it all.
Fear has taught me that.
And you'll never know.
I'll offer a smile if you ask,
"Are you alright?",
I might even nod.

Can you see through the bruises?

Sometimes I Stand Still

When you're little
The world is a big place,
And so are the people.
It's hard to think about later on,
Let alone about tomorrow.
That's such a big idea,
Too big for me to think about.

Now is all that matters,
Now is all that counts.
Sometimes my life stops.
It stands still, right next to me.
I stand still,
Frozen in time,
Frozen in the now,
Motionless,
Emotionless,
Noiseless.

A mist descends in my mind's eye
And silence enters.
It's like I have to catch my thoughts
And shuffle them in my head
To try to understand,
As best I can,
What's going on.

When I freeze,
I can't move,
I become my statue shell.
My body feels too heavy,
My feet refuse to move,
They can't move,
They're stuck,
And the floor holds on to me,
Won't let me go.

Inside I'm frightened,
So very frightened,
And so, I stand still.
Only my eyes and ears stay awake.

My head, always tilted to the right,
Mouth slightly ajar,
Lips parted,
The tip of my tongue protruding,
Just visible on my bottom lip.

An expression steals upon me,
And settles on my face.
My brow furrows,
Pain enters my eyes,
And I stare.
Sometimes I rock from side to side,
Gently swaying to a rhythm
Only I can hear.

Interrupted,
Startled by her snarl,
Words are screamed,
Spittle sprays onto my face:
"Look at ye, look at ye!"

I try to shrink,
I wish I was smaller.
"Ye look like one of them 'nutters'
With ye gob open like that,
Staring like a loony!"

I don't understand
All her angry, shouty words,
Their reasons,
Their hatred,
Or why they're said.
I just know I have to shut them out,
And activate my invisible shield.

I try to disappear inside me,
But my nemesis persists,
Interrupting me this time,
Not just with words and phlegm,
But with blows from
Her fist, her feet, her sticks,

Anything to break me.

I've shut down, switched off,
Trying not to feel,
I don't want to feel anymore,
'Cos that only hurts.
It reminds me of who I am,
Of what I am,
Of everything I'm not,
Of all I can never be.

The world moves around me,
Confusing me, yet somehow
I've got to make sense of what I can
see,
Of the noises I hear,
Of what I can feel
Of what I think.

My body succumbs to her fist, her
foot,
To whatever is offered.
It doesn't flinch anymore,
It embraces the violence,
It has no choice.
And I watch bits of 'me'
Break into pieces,
And scatter.

At least I know I'm worth something.
That's got to be the point, hasn't it?
In these moments I take my mind
away,
I have to, it's best that way.
I call it my 'dream travel',
'Cos that feels good to me in my
world.
It makes me feel better,
And I don't scream anymore,
And I don't cry.
Only my insides have tears,

'Cos I've lost myself,
And soon it will be over.

Sometimes I stand still

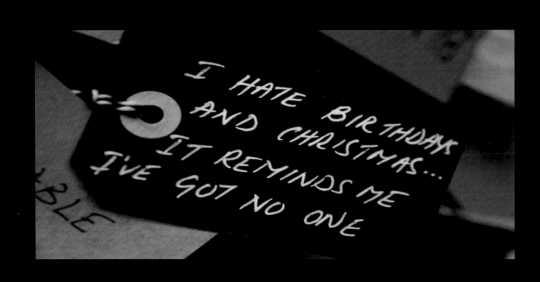

Hurtday

What days?
Birthdays?
We don't get those days.
Ignored days,
Bypassed days,
'Heathen' days,
Our days.

Birthdays?
My shame-day!
It never should have happened day!
"Why would we celebrate a day for you?
You're not worth it".
A not worth it candle,
On a not worth it cake,
On a not worth it day,
For a 'not worth it'!

They wouldn't lower themselves to utter
One uplifting whisper of,
'Happy Birthday to You'.
Those ornery black clad, sap suckers,
Cluck, cluck!
Birthday?
No, Hurtday.

No Colours for My Coat!

Bloody Joseph!
Lucky bloody Joseph, look what he got!
Oh! And we all had to sing about it too!
His amazing technicoloured coat.

And what did we get?
What did I get?
I got a coat made of fuckin' labels!
We all got one here,
One size, extra large,
'Cos you've 'gotta' grow into it.

I don't remember where mine came from,
How I even got it. I never asked.
I just remember they said,
"We can measure the man".
But I was only little.
I'm a boy. I ain't that big.

Labels verbally stitched on,
Loud threads used to secure them
So everyone could hear.
No colours for my coat!

Invisible stitches, mentally sewn,
Indestructible, no matter how hard I tried.
They're stuck now,
And I can't seem to rip 'em off.
They're mine, mine for keeps.

I had to wear my coat like the emperor,
But, unlike him, I was aware.
I felt the stares,
I felt the intent,
I felt the words,
I felt the shame,
My shame.
It was my fault!
Everyone reads 'em,

These labels.
People even believe 'em,
Even add to them.
And I do, most of the time,
'Cos it's all I know.
And sometimes,
I try to put a little word on for me,
A nice word, 'summat' good,
But I ain't getting those ones to stick.
They fall on the floor.
Scattered, they get swept away,
Just like my feelings.
All I know is it means
I can't have,
I mustn't have,
I can't want,
I ain't getting,
I'm a bad 'un, a wrong 'un,
I'm just not good enough.

I wore my coat of labels,
Full of your words,
Your beliefs, your ideals.
Descriptive words meant to keep me in
my place,
Words meant to define me,
To determine my fate,
To secure your expectations of my future,
Fodder for the outside world, the factories,
The prisons, the hospitals, the park
benches.

But inside my pocket
I put my own scraps of paper,
Caught before the wind took 'em away.
My words, my dreams,
And I turned them over in my hand,
"Don't define me,
I will choose who I want to be."

P.YUSUF

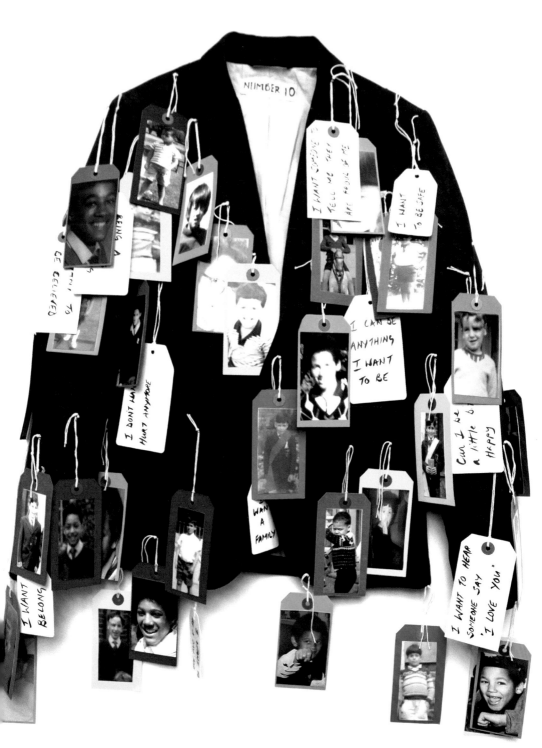

P.yusu

I'M DIRTY

YOU WASN'T WANTED

WORTHLESS

CHILDREN LIKE YOU ARE WRONG .... JUST WRONG

BASTARD

EVIL BOY

It's your own fault you wasn't wanted

FILTHY

FOREIGN LOOKS

I'M SO FULL OF BADNESS

ALL GOOD CHILDREN GO TO HEAVEN .... JUST NOT YOUR KIND

LIAR

UNLOVEABLE

A Moloch's Kiss

She spat on me...at me,
All the while screaming,
"Ye're nothing more than a dirty animal,
Ye deserve nothing less!"
Words of comfort offered to me
Between her punches,
Between her kicks,
Her curses resounding in my head.
"No wonder ye wasn't wanted!"
She told me,
Hysterically laughing
Whilst she dragged me by my hair
To the workroom where clothes are repaired,
But never children!

"No one could love ye,
No one would want the likes of ye.
Ye disgust me!"
The rhythm of the cane echoes her words
As it beats out her songs.
Its notes leave indentations on my little body,
Like lines of an unfinished symphony.
Her words, sealed by her phlegm, her kiss,
As it strikes me with the accuracy of intent.

Each word now anchors itself to my being,
Burning, stinging, penetrating my mind,
My heart, and my soul,
Creating my very own cloak of shame.
She's never once told me I could be loved,

She's never once said I was loved.
She never said!
Instead, always reminding me
Why no one would,
Why no one could.
And I don't get why?
What have I done?

She taught me that I must be bad,
And I deserve my lot.
My crime, she said, was my birth,
My crime, the product of sin!
My reward was being left here, she said,
A reminder for others to view,
To laugh at, to stare at, to pity,
To donate for a worthwhile cause,
But not for me!
A test for her patience, that's what I am.
A test to show her a route into heaven.
My purpose in life!

Never a hug, or embrace of affection,
Never a kind word or praise,
Or anything to make me feel good about myself.
Only her words, her spit, her Moloch's kiss,
Her legacy, and my hurt.
It makes me very sore inside,
My reminder that I exist.
Her marks don't show, no one can see them,
But I still scrub at them, 'cos I feel 'em burn,
I feel their intent,
I feel her kiss!

Have you Ever?

Have you ever:
Opened your eyes from slumber,
To be greeted by despair,
Disappointment, disenchantment,
Realising, you're still alive?

Prayers, I mean real heartfelt prayers,
Went unheard, unanswered.
Fear, panic, terror, dread
Re-enter your being
As you greet the new day,
Your daily breakfast.

Have you ever:
Been battered, beaten so hard,
So mercilessly,
That you no longer care?
Curled in a foetal ball,
Alone with your thoughts,
Your unspoken words,
As blow upon blow strikes you;
Pain becomes your barometer of life,
As it measures their intensity.

Eyes become glazed,
No longer looking,
No longer seeking,
No longer searching.
No longer feeling,
Knowing help isn't coming,
Knowing this is yours to deal with alone.

Have you ever:
Dreaded a door closing behind you,
A body pressed against you,
Hot breath, putrid stench,
Rough hands, manic laughter,
Whispered tones?
So powerless, so small,
Your will crushed.
Submission is your survival.
It's the only way out.

No choice,
No words cried out.
Silent screams,
Silent tears.

Have you ever:
Been spoken to, spoken at,
Like you don't exist,
Don't count, don't matter?
Words spat over you,
On you, striking you
With their depth of
Meaningfulness,
Spitefulness.
No contribution sought.
Decisions made,
Intention stated,
All in your best interest,
Or so they say.

Have you ever:
Had your feelings,
All your spoken dreams,
Taken one by one
And crushed, squashed,
Ridiculed with no remorse?
A perverse pleasure taken
As each one is shattered,
Then smashed,
Whilst inside you're breaking,
So very fragile,
As feelings of hopelessness take hold.

Your persecutors, unrelenting,
Continue with their destruction,
Like vultures picking, pecking,
Scrapping over what remains
Of your fractured self,
Your shattered hopes.
And you must wait,
Until they've finished.
Will they ever?

Have you ever:
Wanted the day to end,
Hoping today was your final sunset,
As you feel nothing matters,
You don't matter,
No longer caring
Because no one cares for you?
When a word like suicide isn't known
Nor understood, but its meaning,
And all it stands for
Is your desire.
Feelings of hopelessness,
Sadness and self-pity
Fuel these thoughts.
So fearful and mindful
That you have to negotiate the night-
time alone,
Knowing the unwanted visitors
Are not just nightmares,
But your reality.

Have you ever:
Clung on to that last bastion of hope,
Reaching down to the depths of your soul,
To find some semblance,
Or a memory of your past
Where innocence exists
And childhood is a long sunny day?
Was there any laughter?
Can you remember?
And remembering this,
That moment
Sustains you,
Regenerates you,
Keeps you alive,
Lets you breathe,
Feeds your dreams.
It becomes your hope.

Have you ever:
Wanted, craved or hungered
For something, or someone,

So much that the thought alone
Made you cry from the inside out?
And the pit of your stomach
Retracts in pain,
Tightening and squeezing
Every breath of desire.
That hurt is very real.

My body is left trembling,
Fatigued, exhausted,
Curled up in a ball,
So small,
Awaiting their strike,
Their kick,
So I can roll away.

Have you ever:
Imagined a day, just one day,
Where you could run,
Skip, jump, laugh
Without a care in the world,
Knowing reprisals aren't lingering?
Stretching out your arms to touch the sky
And stroke the wind,
Letting it gently caress your fingers
As you release balloons filled with all
your hurt,
Watching them soar,
Higher and higher until they disappear.

Marvelling at the sun
Painting colours across a stream,
Then feeling the coolness of the water,
As it tickles your dangling feet.

Holding a hand that fits yours,
Softly, it tenderly offers reassurance.
The warmth of eyes smiling just for you,
Embracing you to your very core.

Have you ever?

Shadow Friend

My closest ally,
My treasured companion,
My trusted confidante,
And sometimes my only friend.

Always with me,
Always by my side,
A protector of secrets,
My secret keeper,
Who showed me I could disappear,
Although I was still there.

Our conversations
Are always one sided,
But I'm listened to
Even when I whisper.
I offer no explanations,
I don't have to,
I don't need to.

I speak the way I can,
The only way I know.
He doesn't mind my edges,
He doesn't judge me.
He just stays there,
Mirroring me,

Never commenting,
But accepting me,
Liking me,
Sitting with me,
And listening,
Just listening.

On sunny days,
He becomes alive.
Mingling with others,
He seizes the chance to dance.
He becomes the child I cannot be,
Without embarrassment,
Without the mantle of shame.

He never shies away from me,
Nor pushes me away.
Never laughs at me,
Nor ridicules me,
Nor teases or beats me.
Instead, he stays with me,
Is loyal to me, just me,
Never letting me down.
Side by side,
Always side by side,
My side!

94

White Boy

Hey 'White boy', 'White boy'!
What do you see?
He looks at his reflection,
It's staring back at him.
His comb rhythmically goes in and out,
Picking, pulling, teasing his curls.
In unison his other hand gently pats his hair,
Shaping, firming, moulding its style,
A perfect 'fro.
My mother's white. So am I.
His thoughts deceive his eyes.
A distorted picture, a blurred vision,
Created and fuelled by their spoken words,
Their sneers,
Their stares,
Their blame,
And their projected shame.
He doesn't want a part of that,
It reminds him that he's bad!
My mother's white. So am I.
Hey 'White boy', 'White boy'!
What do you see?

Number 10

Others have property declaring:
This Belongs to ...
It states their name.
I've seen it!
Written inside out-dated annuals
Donated in boxes for the orphanage.

But that must only be for 'day kids',
Never for the likes of me.
I ain't got anything that says its mine,
I ain't got nothing to say I belong to.
I'm just Number 10.

We've all got numbers here.
What's in a name if it ain't got no use?
And anyway, they can change it if they want to.
We've got no say, we've got no choice,
And sometimes we don't even know.
They take things away when we're not looking,
Or when we're sleeping.

Numbers mark us out,
They notate our clothes,
Our shoes, our flannels, our towels,
Even our 'Gibbs' toothpaste tin,
So no-one can nick 'em.

And sometimes they're used
To count the number of strikes,
But mostly those numbers are exceeded.

Number 10, I'm number 10.
I wish I was Number 1.

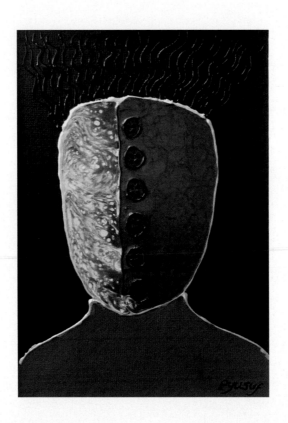

What are You Then?

"Where are you from?"

Are they asking,
Or making a statement?

They don't really look at me,
Their eyes prove that.
Words flow out of their mouth,

"Oh, you're from a home, I see."

See what?
What do you see?

"Hmm, what did you do that was so bad?"

I shrug,
"Nothing."

"Huh! You must have."

"Guess I was born!"

"Nah! Children like you are wrong,
Just wrong."

"I suppose so," I whisper.

"Well, look at you!
What are you?
Wrong!
You just don't belong."

'Cos I Care

I traced 'Someone must love me' in the dirt.
Crouching on my haunches
My arms hug my knees coloured by the dirt.
A stick, dragged along, forming each letter in the earth,
Creating clumsy looking words,
'Cos I can't feel 'em in my heart.

The clouds cry their tears,
My words merge,
Washed away,
Each letter splattered with droplets
Creating a muddy puddle.
Mini streams took away my hope.

I carved the letters 'I matter' into the bark of a tree.
I chiselled that someone 'loved' me.
I even drew a heart around it,
And initialled it.
I dug 'em in deep,
Leaving parts of me embedded
In its gnarled membrane.

My testimony to say, 'I woz ere',
Believing its longevity would strengthen my words.
But my tree was cut down,
A stump is all that remained,
And my words drifted upwards
As smoke from a burning log.
No-one will read them now!

I wrote a small letter to me,
Just a little note.
I didn't have a stamp,
And I don't know if I spelt all the words right.
The teacher said I wasn't the best at spelling or writing,
She thinks I'm dumb!
I addressed it to me.
I even put my Number on it!
That's what I'm known by,
They don't always use my name,
Just Number 10, 'cos we've all got numbers here.

Stretching on my toes to post it in a red chamber,
I can only just about reach its dark mouth.
To have a letter for me would be…
Would be the best thing ever.
It'd make me feel someone cares,
I'd be special, at least for one day.
The thought made me feel warm,
But the postal system by me ain't no good,
'Cos I'm still waiting for it.

I shouted, I screamed,
I whispered,
I cried into the wind
And with the wind.
I do that a lot.
I tell it my dreams, all my wants,
My pain, my hurts, my anger,
My fears and all my secret worries.

And I sit, and I listen for answers
As it deliberates,
Chewing over each of my words,
Thoughts and hopes,
Encircling me, deciding its course, its speed,
Its journey, its replies…
But nothing,
Nothing!
Even the wind doesn't care.

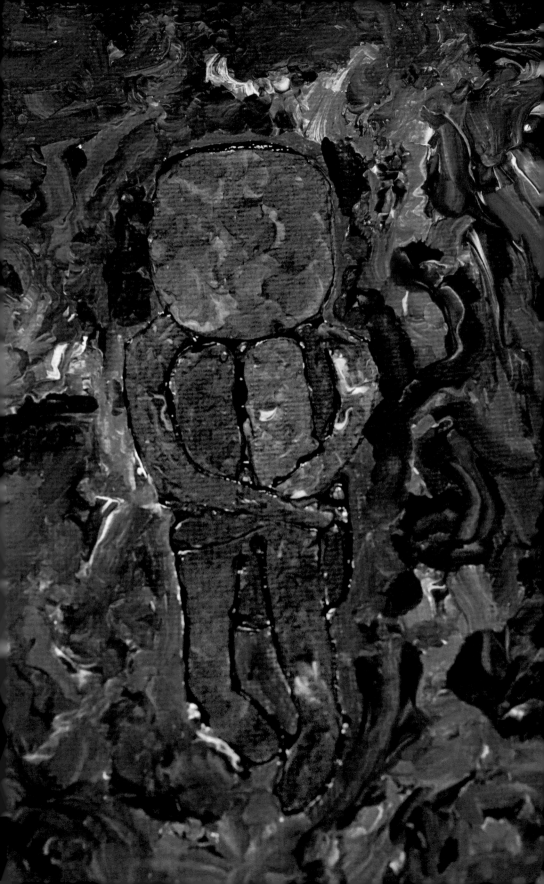

I threw stones.
Each one carried a word spat out by
them,
A bad word about me,
Said about me,
For me,
To me!
And I never once asked for 'em!
I threw them against walls with such
force,
My face scrunched in anger, tear-
stained,
Dirty track lines marking their passing,
Hoping they'd break, splinter into a
million shards,
Never to be fixed, so I could stop
believing all their hate.
But they ricocheted and I had to dodge
'em.
I'm still afraid of being hurt.

I stopped speaking.
My voice just went away,
It became silent,
I think it stopped working!
I guess I must've lost it or something,
And anyway, nobody heard me,
No-one listened to me,
So, it doesn't really matter.
But I still hear my voice in my head,
I can still hear my words,
I can still feel my words,
I still speak to me,
For me,
'Cos I care.

If someone believed me,
Maybe talked with me,
Listened to me with their eyes
And saw me through their ears,
Understood me a little,

Just a little of my world,
And helped me understand me,
Then, I might even like me.
I might begin to believe in me.
I might even begin to trust,
And maybe tomorrow
Have something I can hold onto.

Just Once

Just once
It would be nice to be asked,
How did you do?
Are you any good at that?
What do you think?
What do you want?
It would be nice to be asked,
Just once.

Just once
It would be nice to be told,
Wow, you're good at playing sport,
Don't you read beautifully,
You're so clever, so smart,
I think you're lovely!
It would be nice to be told,
Just once.

Just once
It would be nice to be allowed to say,
I feel sad,
I'm angry,
I'm lonely,
I'm afraid.
It would be nice to be allowed,
Just once.

Just once
It would be nice to feel
Like I belong,
Like I matter,
Like I'm wanted,
Like I'm loved.
It would be nice if I could feel this,
Just once.

Blue nylon rope,
Offering it's everlasting embrace,
holding you firmly,
tightly,
and never letting go....
An intimacy
denied to you as a child.
Something you desperately craved for
now wrapped around you,
so you can touch the breeze.
Gently rocked,
easing you to your final lullaby.
Softly, gently squeezing,
easing all your pain away.
Cut free, it falls into it's coils,
ready to offer it's solace,
.... for its next victim.

Rooter Boy

Under a bridge was where they found you,
Swaying gently in a rhythmic lullaby.
Your final act of bravery, despair, hope,
Now drained from you.
The breeze caressed your face,
Wiping the tear tracks that
Smudged your beauty,
Holding you in a tight embrace,
An act denied you as a child.

In the stillness,
The birds lament your passing,
Their songs offered to the skies.
A calmness surrounds you
Amidst the panic as they lower you,
Removing the blue nylon rope
From your neck,
Its imprint still clinging to your body,
Marking its last gasp of life.
Serenity has descended
And entered your being.
You can rest now Rooster.

The sermon talked of understanding,
Of forgiveness for you,
But you don't need forgiveness.

We all knew who the 'hangmen' were,
Those who were culpable,
Those who should have known better.
They might as well have bought the rope,
They might as well have tied the rope,
They might as well have pushed you.
Their words, their actions
All contributed to your final breath.

Their spokesperson talks almost lyrically,
About how they did so much for you.
Sadly, actions never afforded you in life.
They buried you like a pauper,
Your grave shared with another
Whose fate was determined
By the same system of care.
Intent on forgetting you walked this earth,
You were denied the dignity of a
headstone,
Something tangible to remind us,
Words to acknowledge your existence,
Your life.

You were ours Rooster,
One of us.
We will never forget.

Foster Kid

We've got the perfect place for you!
A shrug is the most I can muster.
'Gotta' go wherever they put me.
Don't get asked.
My voice is a distant echo,
Heard, but never listened to.
They always know best!
'He's just a kid,
A kid in care,
A foster kid.'
Another label, my label,
To be boxed, categorised and catalogued.
Ticks against the list of life options,
I don't count, I'm just a number,
Society's shameful secret,
A hidden statistic
Churned out to fund crusades
To promote their selfish aims.

Like a book with well-thumbed pages,
The paragraphs and chapters are
Unrecognisable to me.
They'll ask me about my story,
But I don't know it anymore.
The lines of my story have been
written by you,
My contribution is minimal.
It's a story of others' opinions and
assumptions,
By which I'm judged.

My eyes close, I've turned away.
I don't hear their voices.
They still keep asking me things.
Their need to persist seems to fill
Some personal gain:

'I really care, I want to help you.'
Good intentions,
Meaningless gestures,
Meaningless words.
It's just a means to an end now.
They don't get that I don't care;
The system lost me a long time ago.
Belief in them, belief in me,
Was just a passing phase,
It didn't linger,
Shadows of bureaucracy saw to that.

They have nothing to offer me,
It's just their job.
They'll move on,
New faces will be offered.
No choice for me.
I'm not even worthy of a goodbye!

What do you want back from me?
Gratitude?
I know one day I'll escape this madness,
I'll make decisions for me,
And that's okay.
I can live with that.
Control will be mine to explore.
I'll join the fringes of society,
Blend into the shadows,
Merge into the edges where it feels safe.
I'll feel safe.
I won't need to explain,
No questions asked,
I'll live a life of sorts,
Get to scratch the itch in my head
And have time to figure stuff out.

The Expert on Floors and Halls

It's so loud, noisy, quiet.
Different voices,
All talking about me, over my head.
They discuss me like I don't exist;
Perhaps I don't.
Maybe it doesn't even matter.

"Oh, he's had a difficult time...
Hasn't washed for ages...
It might be the first thing you do...
Get him into some clean clothes."
But I smell of home.
I know there!
"He doesn't say much,
Probably shy. Aren't you?
"Sorry! He's only got one bag of stuff.
Travels light, don't you?"
I say to myself,
I'm not staying long, you'll see.

Here, everything is bright,
Here everything looks clean.
It smells different.
Eyes are watching me,

Searching me,
For what?
Keep quiet,
Don't say a word,
Don't look up.

The floor has interesting patterns.
I'm an expert on floors and hallways.
Tiles, carpet, wood, you name it,
I've seen 'em all before,
Interesting colours,
Swirls, patterns and stains.
I stroke the walls,
I like stroking walls,
They feel real to me.

Some halls are small, long,
Some are square, massive,
Some are so grand and big
I feel even smaller,
Less significant.
Lots of doors.
Where will they lead?

Stolen Tears

I made myself a vow one day,
No more tears.
Never, never, would I cry again.
The bastards, the bitches,
They can do what they like,
But I won't entertain them.

Let 'em believe they've beaten me,
Let 'em think they've won.
Never will I let them see
My terror,
My fear,
My fright,
My me.

My hurt won't satisfy you,
I'll be the master of disguise;
An illusion is all you will see.
You call it defiance,
The work of the devil,
But they're just words,
Your words.

Your cruelty knows no limit,
The strike of your belt,
Your sticks,
Your fists,
Your keys.
This abuse,
Though consuming,
Will pass.

But the penetrating words,
Designed to infiltrate,
To wreak havoc,
To destroy from inside out,

Are stored away
As reminders of what I am.

Then the shame,
Layer upon layer
Woven by you
Into the fabric of my being
To make me believe
No-one cares,
Could care,
Would ever care.

A heavy cross to carry
On my little shoulders.

That was then.
I'm an adult now,
And I mourn for my lost childhood.
Tears flow from the depths
Of my damaged soul,
Stolen tears
Now seeking their release,
Reliving my childhood,
Revealing my pain,
Expressing the wrongs,
Reconciling me with myself.

My feelings, my thoughts,
And the shame you created
Made me lose sight of me,
Of my belief,
Of my dreams.
And I cry for that boy
Because I cared,
He mattered,
He was important to me.

NAME:

A Stranger Who Knew

A stranger,
He stood, tall and straight,
He held my eye,
He looked at me,
He looked inside me.

He spoke with a softness,
He spoke with such strength,
But with gentleness too.
His voice sang with passion,
It spoke with conviction,
It uttered the truth,
A truth that was lived,
A truth he lived.

He told me his story.
He talked of his life,
What he saw,
What he felt,
How he still feels.
And his words struck a chord,
Shook me inside and out.
His words spoke to me,
Just to me.
He spoke my story,
My story,
My me.

He gave a voice to my pain.
He spoke my hurt,
And gave the gift of words to me.
He let me hold these words,
Touch these words,
And feel their intent.
He held my hand as I
Mouthed these words.
Then he took the words,
Set them free,
And let me watch them
Fly away.

He spoke my darkest despairs,
Buried deep within.
He spoke my pain,
He felt my pain,
He understood my pain,
And he knew.
He knew my private thoughts,
My private me,
My hidden me,
The me behind the smile,
The me behind the tears,
And I smiled through my tears.

I Cried Today

Tear spills...
I cried today.
My vow of silence,
Kept so safe, so hidden,
It's broken now.......and the tears flow.
They pour freely,
Released from their chamber,
And they won't stop.

Unable to stem the flow,
Now I've begun to let go,
And I don't want to.
I watch the lake of childhood,
My childhood,
Expand, grow wider,
Grow deeper, grow darker.
The 'me' no-one knew is exposed,
The key to my inner sanctum discovered,
And the dam to my soul's river opened.

I wail, I weep, I scream.
My voice echoes in stereo,
Reverberating,
Ricocheting off the walls,
And I shed tears for the little boy I
once was,
For the little boy who was me.
My protests were never heard.
No-one was listening,
No-one listened,
No-one ever heard me.

My voice disappeared.
It got lost in their violence,
And I learned to be quiet.

I discovered silence.
I found stillness and comfort
In the shadows with those who feared
life.

I mourn for that boy,
I mourn for that lost childhood,
My lost childhood,
Taken from me,
Stolen, destroyed, defiled,
With only the shadows to keep me safe.

My inner pain is so violent,
I'm shaking desperately
As my nightmares revisit me.
I steady myself.
I need to hold myself and rock,
That's all that can comfort me
In this moment.

An offer to be held isn't wanted,
It's not needed at this time.
I can't cope with that level of intrusion,
That intimacy.
The pain is mine alone.
I have to cope,
I need to.
I need to feel it, to soothe it,
I need to own it, to release it.
I need to comfort my inner child,
The little boy who still lives in me.
He needs me.
We need each other now.
So I cry and I cry.

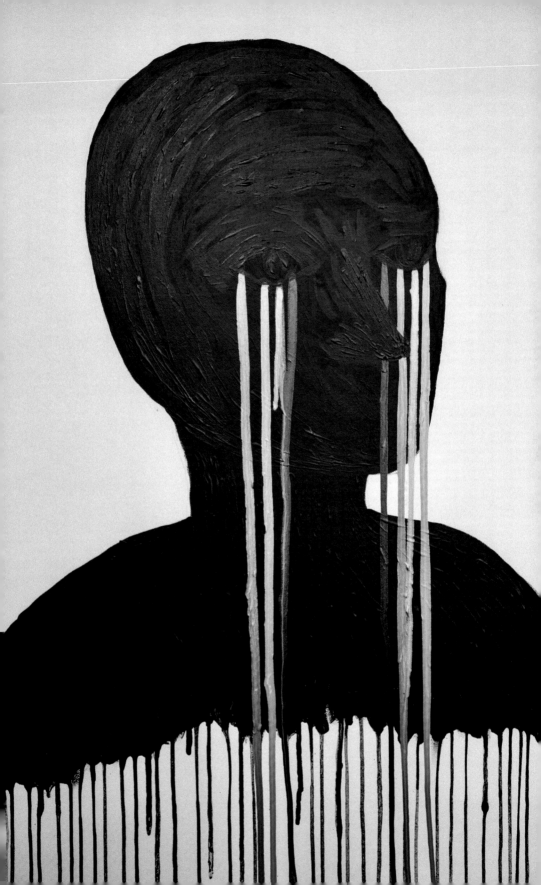

Let it All Go

The sense of relief,
The heaviness...lifted.
I've let go,
Tears flow,
Pouring out
For a childhood lost.

My body lurches,
Stuttering, jerking in fits and starts,
Heaving, trembling, shaking.
It wails, moans, screams,
Lamenting my lost innocence,
My gifted sadness,
Discordant, mournful,
Melodic.

As the emotional burden
Evaporates from my body,
A new strength flows through me,
Filling my veins, giving me life,
Allowing my voice public release,
Ejecting my torment,
Eradicating the disease that festered,
The disgust,
The consequence
Of growing up in care.

Look at me now!
I'm smiling.

I Can Dream at Night

Nightmares don't knock
On my door anymore.
I've chased them away.
A calm has settled,
I've found myself,
I've found my child within.
And he's safe now.
No more storms raging inside
To startle me awake,
To make me fear the night.
Instead, I'm allowed to sleep now,
And, finally, to dream.

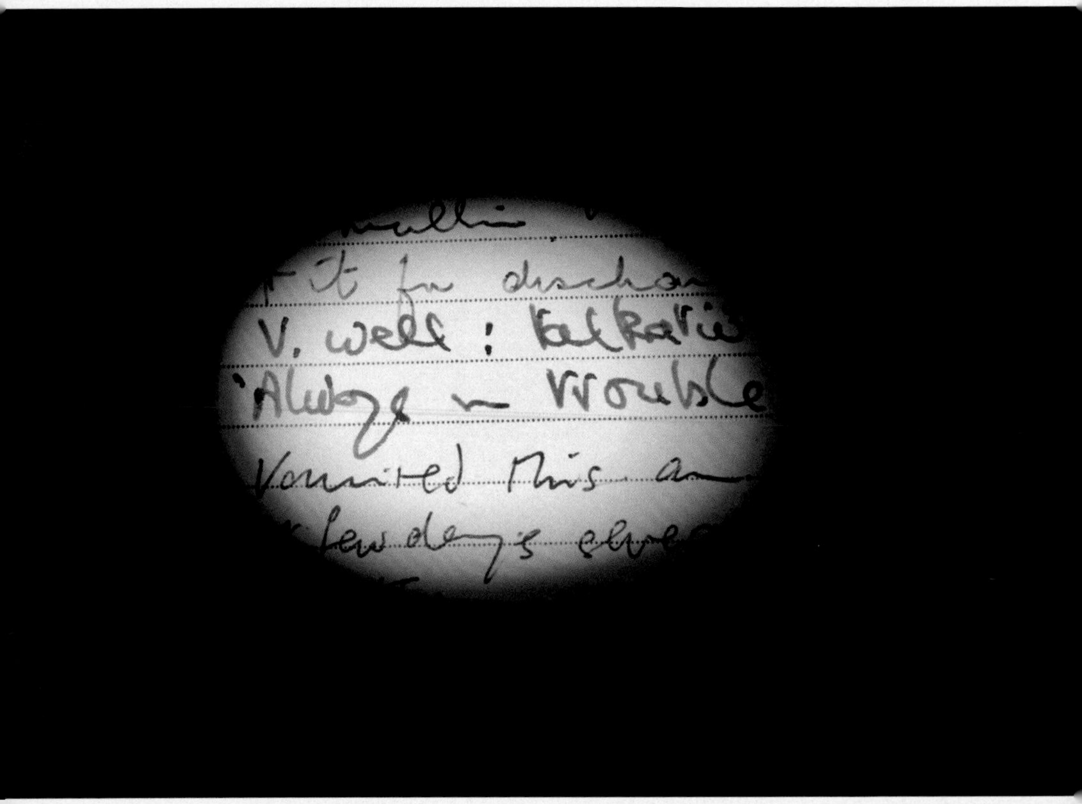
V. well :
'Always in trouble
Vomited this
few days

This Boy is Always in Trouble

My file:
Discoloured sheets of paper,
Lying randomly across one another,
Page numbers out of sequence,
No order; mixed up.
A contemptible file
Fashioned by those
Who claimed they cared.

My childhood life lies before me.
Gaps, gaps, I'm not complete.
Years have passed without any notes.
Did I even exist!
Didn't I mean something, anything, to
anyone!
Was I that insignificant?

Important events are missing,
Events to tell my story,
To speak of things I did,
To speak of me.
Missing pieces, unwritten sentences
That reflect a missing childhood.
Convenient, treachery, it stinks of
conspiracy.
From age 5 to 11 I don't exist!
I don't exist!

No entry except one,
This boy is always in trouble,
Written on a medical document
In the familiar doctor's scrawl.
Nothing else.
A statement,
One line,
Always in trouble.

No notes or records of
My broken fingers,
Or my burns,
The burns to my hands,
The burns to my arm
That you inflicted.

My defilement? No mention.
Just, this boy is always in trouble.
The doctor treated me,
I remember.
I remember my pain,
I remember my screams,
I can still hear them!
Mostly though, I remember the shame
That I had to carry by myself,
Always by myself.
And you all watched.
Oh yes,
He's a good Catholic doctor,
A great man,
That's how you saw him.
You even made me pray for him.

He tutted,
Oh! It's him again,
What's he done now?
Complicit in your silence,
Complicit in your beliefs,
He doesn't really matter,
He wasn't wanted in the first place!
He's a strong lad, he'll get over it.

Did I like balloons?

I hate it when they talk about families,
The past,
And guess the baby picture.

I hate it when they reminisce,
About holidays, places they've been,
Things they've done.

"Do you remember the time I tripped and fell in the pool?
Or when you dressed up and sang 'I'm a little tea pot'?
Do you remember how granny would sing and dance with you?"

Shut up! Shut up!
I want to say.
Not everyone knows their story.

My past is sketchy,
Cloudy, a jumbled puzzle.
It feels like I've always been as I am.

There are things I don't want to recall,
Sad things, painful things, things that hurt,
Things I can't remember, or don't want to remember,
But there are things I wish I did.

When did I walk, talk?
Did I laugh a lot?
Was I good at anything?
Did I like peas?
Was I happy?
Did I like balloons?

I just don't know.

Look at Me Now

Go on, look at me!
Look at me now,
I dare you!

I don't have to look away.
I'm not that little boy anymore.
The shadows don't make me jump.

I no longer have to feel shame,
I no longer have to feel guilty,
I no longer need to blame myself,
I no longer need to be grateful....
Grateful for what!

You nearly won,
You nearly crushed me,
Both inside and out,
But you never broke me.

My spirit was strong.
It wanted to live,
It persevered,
It thrived,
Banishing fear,
Banishing shame,
Banishing guilt.
I was never to blame,
I was a child!

Now, I stand here and say,
Look at me!
Go on,
Fucking look at me!
Look at me now,
I dare you!

Yes, I'm angry!
You're damn right,
I'm fucking angry.

Belief in me,
Belief that I meant something,
That's my strength.

It didn't waver,
It walked alongside me,
Day in, day out.

All those innocent lives,
You destroyed them,
Inflicting pain,
Fuelling despair,
Or turning your backs.
You looked the other way,
Ignoring the violence,
Ignoring our hurt,
Culpable in your silence.

Go on,
Look at me!
Look at me now!

You see the man I became,
Not because of you,
No, in spite of you.

Me...
I'm smiling now,
Secure, content, loved.
Yeah! Loved!
Something you said could never happen.

And valued in abundance....
Alien words to your ears.
My head is held high.

You can't hold my gaze.
Your propaganda is disintegrating,
Your lies evaporating in the face of truth.
Truth will always triumph.

Go on,
Look at me!
Look at me now,
If you dare!

Going Back

Standing on the perimeter, the fringes.
Ahead, the ghosts of my childhood.
Deep breathing, fists clenched,
Tapping the sides of my legs.
My mind's eye says, 'It'll be okay',
My voice within reassures me,
Calmly, calmly, inhale deeply,
And exhale,
Creating a rhythm,
I can do this,
I will do this,
I must do this!

I look around searching,
Searching for some memory
Of happy times.
But the buildings are long gone,
Squashed, demolished,
Like my childhood.

I can still see all the children.
I see their pain, their misery,

The despair behind their smiles,
Behind their eyes.

It still terrifies me!
Why? I'm fifty now!
Grown, but in that instance,
That fleeting moment,
I'm five, I'm six, I'm seven,
Scared, confused,
Lonely, frightened,
My pockets full of hope,
Full of dreams.

One big breath,
I move forward,
I step in simultaneously
To my past and my present,
To battle my nightmares,
To attend foster panel,
Because every child matters....
Don't they?

129

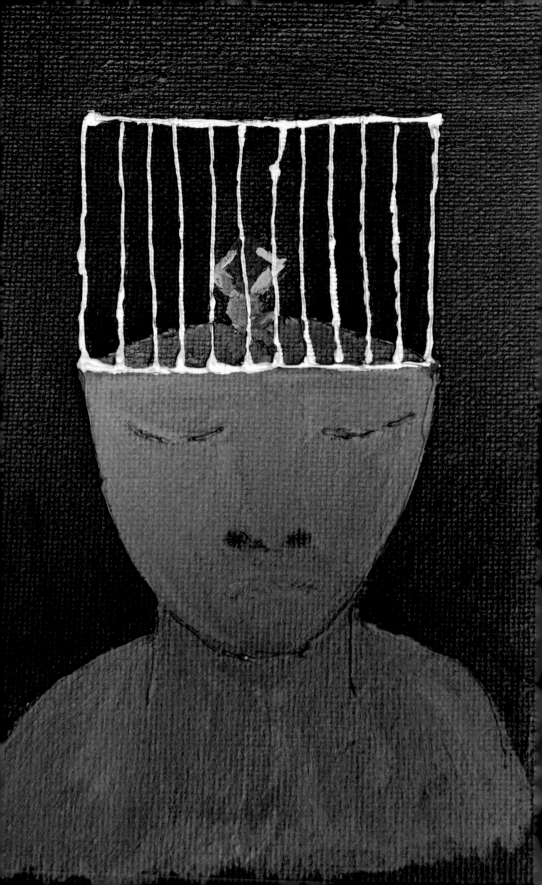

Our Dilemma

What do I do with
All that I know,
All that I've felt,
All that has been done to me?

To speak,
To say what has happened,
Is that enough?

I'm exhausted!
I don't have the fight,
The strength to do more.

Afraid to face my tormentors,
The institutions,
The religious doctrine that guided them;
They hold such power over me still.

Fear so ingrained,
And behind it all lies rejection,
Always rejection,
Bloody rejection.

How can I do more
When others still need protecting?

Not ready to stand up!
Weakened,
So damaged
By the systematic abuse.
The lies, the beatings,
They were all our fault.
We deserved it.

Children like us should be grateful!

Still so frightened,
With feelings of guilt.
Could we have done more to stop things,
To stop the pain, to save ourselves?

I should have done more to protect others,
To protect those who needed protecting.

But we all needed protecting.
Should it have been left to us?

Despicable Me, Despicable You.

A crime to be born, a despicable thing,
Contemptible, loathsome, detestable,
Abhorrent, heinous, abominable,
Repellent, awful and repugnant.
Such big words for a little boy,
I couldn't even pronounce them.
They were your words, your labels.
Oh, despicable me!

You made me pray for forgiveness,
'Cos everything was my fault.
Not only was I dirty and filthy,
But unworthy of kindness or love.
You despised me,
And loathed looking after me.
Do you remember you told me that?
Oh, despicable me!

Do you remember you said I looked
shabby?
That I always looked like a tramp?
A miserable child, so sullen,
An ungrateful child who no-one would
want.

I was rotten through and through.
And I believed your words,
The shame, the blame, the guilt.
Oh, despicable me!

Relentless, persistent, determined,
You broke me as much as you could
With your fists, your boots, your keys,
Your sticks and your words,
Crushing my spirit and body,
Silencing my voice,
And squashing my child.
Oh, despicable you!

People talk about a weight lifting,
When facing their deepest fears,
And I now know this lightness of spirit,
This freedom of body and mind,
As I talk and I write, and I talk and I
cry,
And scream aloud that I mattered,
That I'm worthy, was worthy and
always will be.
Despicable you, not despicable me.

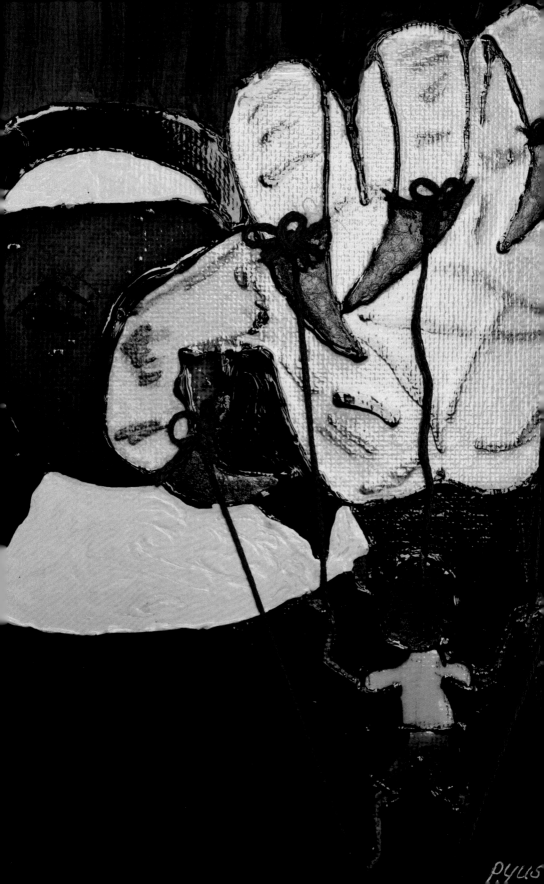

I Am

I am the boy who seized the storm.
I grappled its fierce soul
And tamed it to a gentle breeze.

I am the boy who watched, who stared.
I noticed everything,
And absorbed it all.

I am the boy you fear the most.
I am your guilty nightmare who visits you
Because you chose to do nothing.

In spite of you, I am!

Politician, Politician

Politician, Politician
You'd better start listening
To us, to me.

Your laws made us,
They shaped us, ignored us,
And took us away from all that we knew.

Your laws promised better,
Promised choices and chances,
And more opportunity too.

Politician, politician,
Why do you lie?
Your promises are empty
You simply don't care.

Our backs are presented
To your smiles full of knives,
As you stab and you bludgeon,
And we're sacrificed.

But we know the truth,
That you're letting us down
As we fill up your prisons,
Your hospitals too,
Park benches, shop doorways
And morgues.

Politician, Politician
When will you wake up,
And listen to those who know?

The voice of the child
Who is no less than yours,
And no less deserving of love.

Treasure them, value them,
They have a future,
A future as much as your own.

Politician, Politician
Stand out from the crowd
And listen before it's too late.

Forgotten Promises

Left with the promise of return:

"You'll never be forgotten,
I'll come back,
I'll come back and get you."

Throw away words
For throw away children.
Words with no substance,
Words that weren't meant,
Words that weren't sincere.
Words spoken in fear,
Words laced with guilt.
Words written to appease me,
To give me some hope,
A false sense of security.
Words, that's all they ever were.

My feelings were confused,
Puzzled, reaching out, stretched.
They desperately sought a foothold,
A place to cling onto
In my imaginative mountain range
Of hope and belief.

That's how it felt,
It's how I felt... desperate,
Alone, frightened, scared,
Unsure of what lay in the shadows.
Feelings I learned
And had to embrace,
Became my skins of acceptance
As I navigated the path which lay in
front of me.

Didn't I have to survive!

I covered myself in clothes of muted tears,
Weighed down by my gifted cloak of fear,
Of stigma and shame.
Invisible clothing,
Like the emperor's,

Subjected to mocking tones,
Stares and ridicule.
And hope?
It only stayed with me for a while
Until I buried it deep within,
Replacing it with despair, ambivalence,
Uncertainty and suspicion,
Alertness to danger and reprisals,
And an acceptance of their motives.

We all waited,
Faces pressed against railings,
Watching strangers,
Searching their details in hope,
Willing them to recognise us,
Willing them to see us,
Believing that whispered promise
Would be fulfilled.

You said you'd never forget me,
But I'm still here!
Don't you know where I am?
Can't you find me?
I scream at night!
Can't you hear me?
Can't you feel me?

You'll never be forgotten, you said.
I'll come back, you said.
I'll come back and get you, you said.
Whispered words that plagued my
imagination,
Whispered words that tormented my heart,
Whispered empty words devoid of
meaning.

I waited,
I waited,
I waited...
Nothing!
No answer!
No one came!

Meeting Mother

She didn't hear my abject fear
When I screamed
As she walked away,
Her head bowed,
Never once turning back.
I felt such coldness,
An emptiness,
Where her presence once was,
Its indentation still warm,
The air around it scented,
Filling my nostrils.

I met her again in my twenties.
A surreal experience.
My needs were curious,
I needed to know
I wasn't all bad.

I didn't believe in happy endings.
Hadn't I already been let down before.
A whole childhood of let downs!
So, I wore no rose-tinted glasses that day,
And had no expectations.

Yet I hoped for a connection,
An invisible umbilical cord
Still tying us together.
But it wasn't on offer that day.
Her fear got in the way,
Her need to protect her feelings
Was all I saw.

"I'd have kept you had I known
  You weren't too coloured."
Were her first words uttered!
Not, how are you? or I've missed you,

Nothing from her heart.
Instead, she appeared cold,
Or maybe afraid,
Her protective shield
Shrouding her.
My guard was instantly activated.
Hadn't I been hurt enough!

Our conversation was polite, stilted.
Her eyes only came to life
When she spoke of my father.
She even offered a smile!
"I was charmed by his exotic looks
  And perfect manners."
Her eyes looked upwards,
Searching the skies.
Her hand reached over,
"You have the look of your father."
I moved away.
"I see the same gentleness in you."
And then nothing.

Her expression stiffened,
She didn't want to say more,
And we parted with the promise
To keep in touch,
Only this time
I was able to stand and watch
As she drove away,
On my own again,
But without tears,
Without screaming.
Just a wistful thought,
Did her eyes look back
Through her rear-view mirror?

141

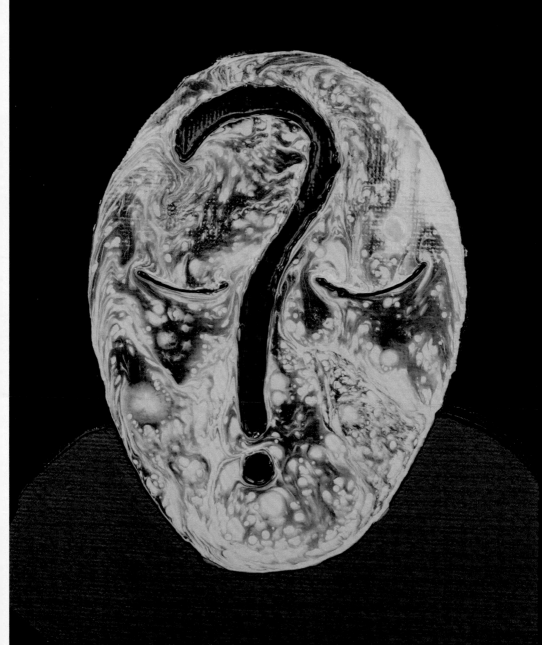

The Other Me

"So, who do we have here?"
I was asked.
In that split second
A moment of hesitation
Sits on my tongue....

Paul, my name's Paul.

I always felt unsure about my name,
It didn't fit,
Like it didn't belong.

I wanted to be Sultan,
Strong, brave,
Powerful Sultan,
Everything I wasn't!

I'm told a mother's voice is heard
Before her infant takes its first breath,
Its first cries.
It knows its mother's story.

Years later, my mother lay in hospital,
Visited by her own mortality.
She announced,
"They wouldn't let me name you after
your dad."

I looked at her,
Hardly daring to draw breath.
She never spoke about him.

"We, ...we wanted to call you Yusuf,
The angel, our angel.
We..."

They were together, I never knew!

"They said it's not in your interest,
A foreign name.

With his looks,
It'll only hold him back."
Now I'm confused,
But remain silent,
Afraid she'll stop.

*"**They** called you Paul."*

There's anger in her words,
I can sense it.

*"**They** chose your name,*
A holy day, a saint's day,
Their order's name.
That was your birth date,
Your birthright."

I detect a hint of sadness,
Remorse even.

She stroked my cheek,
She's never stroked my cheek.
That level of intimacy
Was never afforded to me.

*"**They** called you Paul,*
But you will always be my angel –
Yusuf."

A shadow crossed her face.
I've missed my chance
To ask about him,
What he was like...

I can tell as she turns away
She thinks she's said too much,
But I want more.

A Mother's Blessing.....Not me

I ain't no mother's blessing,
Well, she's never said I was.
I was her shock,
Her shame, her guilt,
Her dark secret,
In more ways than one,
Her unexpected,
Her not wanted.

I get it, that she's still ashamed,
In fact, I know it,
Her eyes tell me every time we meet.
Panic lies behind her stare,
Fearful of what I might say,
What I might ask.

And sometimes I detect sadness,
Hidden in the furthest corners of her
eyes.

Every time we speak, the pretence
begins.
Her voice lacks honest sincerity,
And we just talk through the motions,
Navigating meaningless words,
Polite words,
Forgettable words
Of forgettable conversations.

I'm her reminder, her throwback,
A glance towards her past,
A distant memory to hide away,
If only she could.
A memory of a time she wants no part of,
A time she wishes had never happened,
A time of fear,
Her recurring nightmare.
And I have the nerve to visit!

I am the elephant in the room, her room,
Where she's still afraid,

Afraid she'll be found out,
That the 'bastard' will reveal himself,
Or be revealed,
And then everyone will know.

They'll pick up their biblical stones
And throw at the one
Who committed such a sin,
The sin that was me,
Her sin of lust,
Her sin of passion.

But secretly,
I think she likes the martyrdom.
It's become her silent breath,
It gives her a mental wall to hide behind,
It allows her to be the 'holy' Mary,
Awaiting an anointment,
A blessing from her priest!

She gives herself permission
To ignore what stands in front of her
face.
She doesn't have to face up to the truth.
Her truth, her pretence can remain intact.
It's so easy for her to look away.

Acceptance of me is tainted.
It doesn't really exist,
Except on her terms,
And only her terms.
I don't have a say.

Sometimes I'm an Arab,
Other times a 'Paki',
A half-caste.
My mother says she's confused,
But she knows I'm a coloured (her
words)!
"Not one of hers, but one of them."

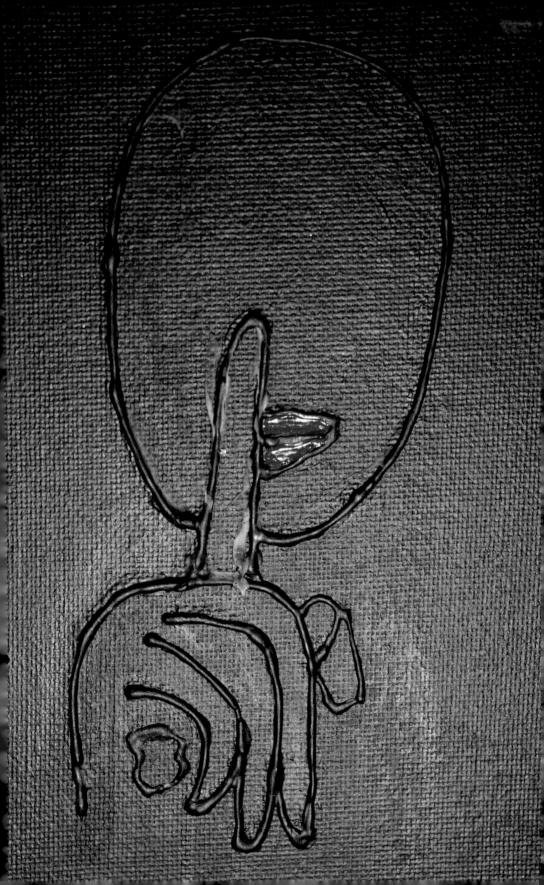

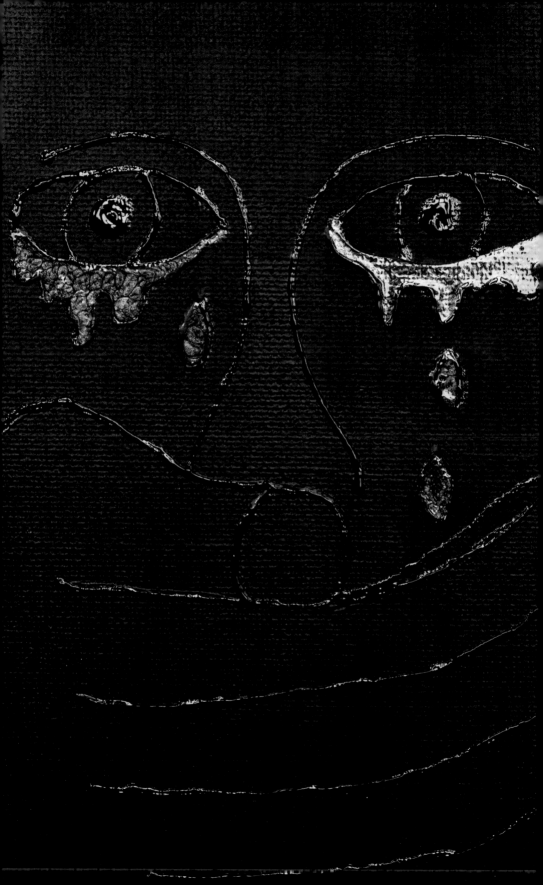

But within her four walls, her domain,
I'm hers.
She even calls me her son, but only for
my ears,
Barely audible as they're whispered
under her breath.

To the rest of the world, to the outside,
To those that ask, to those she
chooses to tell,
I'm just someone she knows,
No connection, no tie, no relation,
Someone she met a long time ago,
Someone who has latched on to her,
Who has no family!
And she, with such a charitable heart,
Offered a sense of family!
Alleluia! Praise the lord!

And, amidst her delusions,
She treats all her 'children' the same.
They're always welcome with open arms,
Day or night, no matter when,
No appointment necessary,
No phone call first to check the coast
is clear,
Just in case!
Fearful still of being alone with me,
And I still don't know why.
She never says.

Never has she asked,
Never, not once,
How were you?
How did you manage?
How did you cope?
Were you happy?
It's as if I never existed before,
I have no past,
I had no childhood.

Never, never has she said,
"I'm sorry".
Never an apology, not once.
Only a dismissive,
"It is what it is."

She told me her feelings come first,
Second, third and last.
She doesn't wish to know about mine.
Words about my feelings only get in
the way.
She bemoans they're aimed to hurt her,
To get back at her.

So, my childish 'tactic' of silence
Has become my option of choice again,
Still mindful of other's feelings, her
feelings,
Gifted to her from me.

My children are told of their genetic past,
A genetic link, a story of a figure
Who is their grandmother,
But no part of their lives.
Her choice!
Their names remain alien to her,
Their birth dates long forgotten.
Interest is mouthed by her,
But holds no depth,
A polite expectation,
Something to fill the voids in
conversation.
She refers to them as, the girl, the boy,
The other fellow, the young one,
And the 'poor little creature'
Blighted by his past,
By his beginnings,
Beginnings akin to mine,
And yet no less part of my family.
My beautiful children,
Each and every one of them.

And yet, when asked about her other
children's children,
She becomes a woman possessed,
Waxing lyrically about all they do,
Of how much she loves them,
Of how much she enjoys them.

Yet still no acknowledgement of mine,
And no recognition of my inevitable hurt.
There was no, "I've thought about you,
I've missed you every day",
No words to convey that I mattered.

And she queries why I no longer visit,
Why I no longer mention their lives.
Her interest is feigned, false,
And lacking in sincerity.

I'm resigned to it now.
To use her own words,
"It is what it is."
It's not that I don't care,
But because I do.
I seek no reconciliation,
No reconnection,
Nor mother's love.
They're not for me.
I accept the way things are.
I can't change the way she is.
It's the best it will be,
And that, I suppose, is something.
I ain't no mother's blessing,
Not me.

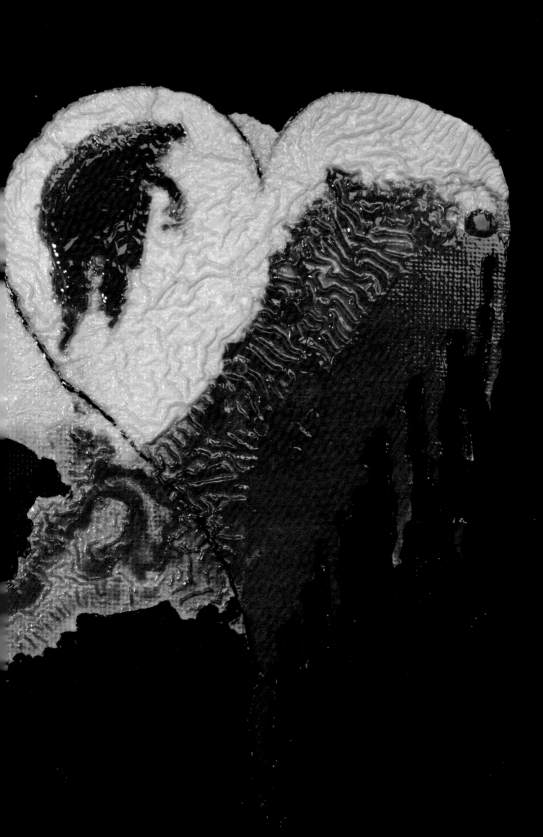

My Feelings Tread So Softly

Despite what you think I feel,
You don't recognise
Or acknowledge
That my feelings
Are mine.

You dismiss them,
Attach no credit to them,
Despise them,
I think you even fear them.

Yet my feelings
Tread so very softly,
Leaving no print,
No marks,
No evidence they have visited.

Do they exist?

Respectful of you,
Not wanting to distress you,
Or even hurt you,
Mindful that your pain is real,
I keep them tucked away,
Hidden in the folds of my soul,
In the cavernous depths of my being.

Fearful to vent them,
Or air them
In case they drown you,
Swamp you,
Crush you with their weight,
Swallow you up,
Or choke you with their unpleasant
taste.
I keep them locked away,
Combination unknown.

My feelings,
I carry them on my own,
Always on my own,
Supressing them,
Taming them,
Tempering them,
Keeping them at bay,
Controlling them,
So that they never spill over,
So that they are never heard.

And from you,
All I ever want is just to be asked,
*"How do **you** feel?"*

I Am Worthy

My spirit's been bruised,
My heart was fractured,
My voice crushed!
They tried to break me,
But I've discovered
A single gold thread of belief.
Locked away
In the deepest
Recess within me
A label freely swings,
And reads,
I AM WORTHY!

Poetry narratives

Paul wrote a number of narratives (which he called preambles) to go with his poems. When we discussed the development of the book, he was clear that he wanted a shortened version of his preambles to be included, but we had agreed that these may be better situated away from the actual poems and artwork. We had toyed with ideas of these being in a separate leaflet to go with the book and were full of ideas about how these might be used. Ultimately, I reached the decision to include them in a short section towards the end of the book. Joanne and I have been unable to locate narratives for a couple of the pieces, so we have written something about our discussions with Paul about the poems. Paul's wife Sarah has contributed to the missing narratives too. Where the words are not Paul's then the narrative is in italics to make this clear and the name of the person who wrote it is included.

Since the poems are in an order to show Paul's journey then to some extent these 'premables' provide the narrative to Paul's life.

1. My Voice, Our Voice (page 33) and 2. My Story (page 35)

These pieces cover the permission I have given myself to explain that it's okay now, it's safe. Saying aloud what happened to me and others who had the misfortune of experiencing growing up as children of the state system during the 1960s and 70s has proven to be an emotional rollercoaster. It has also meant that I have had to face things I'd rather forget or consign to the back of beyond. It means looking at shame in the eyes and stating, "I don't want you anymore".

My greatest personal challenge has been, how much of me do I tell. I have also questioned why tell it now and what will it change? Reflection on these questions has been my supportive ally along the way, allowing me time to think and address these points.

I recognise how I have gained a better sense of who I am and finally understand that I was never to blame. I was a child who had unimaginable things done to him, who felt the gravity of emotional hurt inside him, taking it all to heart and not understanding why or what had he done. I was a child who clung on desperately to a belief that kindness existed and thought about it a lot!

These verses speak of denial, of not being heard, of anger, sadness, fear and the fear of reprisals, the fear of events and my feelings. They also highlight my own growing confidence, and maybe a level of acceptance that I can allow myself to disclose what has occurred. I'm shaking, trembling as words leave my mouth, as my mind erupts, desperate to rid itself of the pain it has held on to. And behind all of them, there is a strength and a grain of belief that somewhere I mattered.

3. The Creation of Me (page 37)

Not having an understanding as to why I was in care only fuelled my imagination with stories that I was here to learn some sort of lesson.

It hurt me when people referred to me as a bastard, even more so because of the stigma that was associated with that word. Initially, my response was to fight, and I lashed out, especially at my peers. As I became older, my way of coping altered, and I responded verbally instead: "Yeah, I might be a bastard but at least I was conceived out of passion." Saying this made me feel better about me.

I wrote the 'Creation of Me' with a poetic eye, incorporating 'snippets' my birth mother offered when she spoke about my birth father. It plays out the scene I imagine took place, and I'll hold onto the fact that I was conceived and created from passion.

4. Firstborn (page 41) and 5. Six Weeks (page 42)

Like a lot of those who became children of the state during the late 1950s, 60s and 70s, I qualified as such due to my illegitimacy, being born out of wedlock, and because I was one of the ever-increasing number of 'brown' babies being born. White women were enticed by the exotic looks and ways of those that had been invited to come to the motherland from all over the commonwealth (my birth mothers take on that time!) Your country needs you, they were promised, and yes, they did, but only to do the jobs that the British workforce didn't want to do. As a result, these people were marginalised and naturally gathered together, and a whole generation of brown and coffee-coloured children were born, much to the horror of the society at that time.

Institutions (mother and baby homes) were set up so these errant women could go away and deliver their bastard children. Most were allowed to stay for six weeks following the birth and then given the opportunity to start afresh, leaving their mistake behind to start life over with the knowledge that their child would be found a good home, a family who would love them and give them everything they couldn't. Knowing this must have comforted some.

Unfortunately, the truth of the matter is that most of these 'brown babies' would languish in institutional care, deemed unadoptable because of their differences, and abandoned to carry the stigma of their birth. Six weeks isn't a long time and the bonds formed only amplified the loss and separation felt by those babies when their mothers were made to leave them behind.

The question I have asked myself many times over the years revolves around what support there was for these women. What aftercare support was offered? Would so many of us have been left if our mothers had known what lay in store for us?

6. Our Mantra (page 45)

Picture if you can, a group of four or five little children, ranging in age from four and a half to six, sitting crossed legged in a line, nudging, shoving each other, desperately raising their hands to be the first to answer the questions being fired at them, seeking the adulation of being heard first, to receive the acknowledgement that they were correct in their response.

These children were so desperate to feel some words of praise that they didn't care or mind the content. And so began, "Our Mantra".

7. Time to Turn Away Child (page 46)

I wrote this with a heavy heart and tears. I recalled a time when, following an incident of abuse by one of the older boys, the nun in charge rebuked me, dragging me upstairs to the work room despite my protest and tears.

Any thought I had in my head of being comforted was swiftly dismissed, as she thrashed the living daylights out of me because as she put it, "Ye are up to no good", whatever that really meant.

Unwittingly, by referring to me as a dirty article, a thing, an 'unhuman', she gave me a 'space' where I could put my physical 'me' into, detaching myself from events as they unfolded.

I recall how I mentally got through that episode, how I gave myself excuses to hold onto, that if I pretend these things aren't happening then they can't be real. It was my way of coping in the best way I could.

8. Cake for Tea (page 49)

St Patrick's day was a big occasion growing up. The children in the homes were encouraged, and made, to celebrate this feast day both for its significance to the Catholic faith in Ireland and in England and for the nuns who were in charge of us. Ninety-nine percent of the nuns and priests in charge of us were Irish, so we were taught that being Irish was a 'great' thing. It was also one of the very few days I saw nuns smiling as they opened cards and gifts sent to them from relations in Ireland.

On this day we were told that we could be Irish, especially as most of us had Irish sounding surnames. We would line up to have shamrock or tricolour flags pinned to our jerseys. We'd be reminded how St Patrick got rid of all the snakes from Ireland and squashed them like heathens, like us, but we didn't care because today was a celebration day. I looked forward to St Patrick's day. It allowed me to belong and identify with a community for a day but, perhaps more importantly for me, it meant that I'd be definitely having cake for tea, and that was always a good thing!

9. A Troubled Child, A Troubled Boy (page 50)

I wrote this after reading the notes written about me as a child. It pained me to recall how I was viewed. I lacked the understanding, the imagination to fight back. My acts of compliance just weren't good enough when those in charge dislike you. I reflect on the whirlwind of confusion and thoughts that filled my mind. My understanding was immature and childlike, unable to see the wider picture. All I wanted or needed was to feel that I mattered.

10. Tuck Shop (page 53)

Saturday mornings were filled with excitement and anticipation. Saturday morning was 'Tuck shop' day! Chores would be completed and inspected by our nun; we would all hope that her high standards had been met. Then she would tell us to line up.

I remember how I and the rest of the children would be made to stand in line, always the big boys in front, with the youngest last in line. Twenty-five boys all eager to get their goodies. Many fingers were crossed, hoping that 'Sister' had forgotten past misdemeanours and we would get away with spending our pocket money this week.

I've tried to convey exactly what was going on and how I experienced the 'tuck shop shuffle' to claim my 'prize'.

It was years later before I began to understand the sadistic behaviour of the 'Sisters' who lulled me so often into a false belief that this time I'd be successful in getting my hands on the prize. Perhaps the most disturbing thing I recall is their insistence that we all queue up and go through the ritual, almost to its completion, before removing the prize with a smile on their face.

11. Zoo Time (page 56)

Picture a coach load of people disembarking outside your front door, being allowed in, able to explore and go anywhere within your home, pulling open drawers, looking in cupboards, examining your personal effects, and not once asking permission. Strangers coming up to you, entering your personal space, touching your stuff, poking you, poking your food, their children giggling, sniggering, pointing at you, laughing at you. People asking personal questions and dismissing your answers. What little possessions we had were fair game to those that attended and would be offered by the nuns with the explanation that, "*It's too much that they have*".

This was our regular Sunday occurrence. We would be told that a 'coach load of the best Catholics' would be coming to look around. Strangely this usually coincided with our teatime. We'd be reminded about being on our best behaviour and to speak only if spoken to, with the veiled threats not to touch or eat any of the extras displayed on our tables (the consequences were widely known!)

The fact that this at least made them feel better about themselves wasn't lost on us. We just learned not to believe in their motives or intentions. For me, the best part of this experience was that the people sometimes looked uncomfortable and therefore only stayed a short time. Phew, what a relief!

12. Look I Can Dance (page 59)

People sometimes talk about the wonder of adoption days and how great it is for potential adopters to experience, meet and see children in their natural environment. It sounds idyllic, yet the reality for the child who isn't selected is devastating. It can confirm and create layers, fuelling a sense of rejection, of not being good enough or as good as another child. You may, therefore, be surprised that a form of adoption day operated during the 1960s, where children like me would be introduced to, and made to dance and perform for, audiences.

We were told that people who wanted to be our mummies and daddies were coming to see us and take us home and we eagerly awaited their arrival, already believing that this time we'd be lucky. The reality was that all the blonde blue-eyed children seemed to disappear, leaving us many 'shaded' children behind. To know I wasn't being selected again was difficult, especially when I'd keep asking if my new mummy and daddy were here, only to be told I wasn't wanted again! It didn't help with the way I felt about myself.

'Look I Can Dance' is my attempt to put into words how I felt, how my face of expectation and hope eventually stopped looking upwards, and I sought self-protection in the shadows.

13. Another Day...Another Year (page 60)

Growing up in care is a lonely place. Not understanding the reasons for being there only validates the loneliness and heightens thoughts of not being up to much! Seeing groups of people or individuals viewing children with the idea or intention of perhaps taking one is hard to stomach when you're not chosen again. To 'get it', that you're not wanted at such an early age is devastating. Rejection and a sense of no value or worth become an emotional state of mind, fuelling the loneliness and feeling that no one cares. The only saving grace at the time was that I wasn't alone; so many of us faced another day, another week, another month, another year!

14. Every Day I Write a Letter (page 63)

Like most kids growing up in care I fantasised about my origins. Obviously, I came from royalty and was only here to be taught a lesson. Soon I would be rescued and brought back into the bosom of my family where my earlier experiences would become distant memories. Well, we all have to dream!

In my head I composed so many letters to my mother but, strangely, never my father. Each one was torn up and cast aside. Nothing I thought of could put into words what I desperately wanted to convey. My aim to write the perfect letter eluded me. In fact, when I did trace her, it took me three months to put acceptable words into a letter to her, as I was at pains to show her some sort of compassion for having to leave me behind.

15. You're Not with the Babies Now (page 64)

First days should be special and most of us can remember the first time when My introduction to a children's home in Coleshill initiated the dismantling of my childhood. I was physically and emotionally shocked into a world that was now going to be mine. I had recently moved from another institution to a family who announced that God had told them about a boy nobody wanted. Unfortunately, it also turned out that they didn't want me either!

Aged four and a half, I was given back, only this time I was being sent to another institution for boys.

My first memory of Coleshill was the size of the door at St Edwards; did giants live here? After introductions I was assigned to the 'Cottage Homes' and here my reality waited. Any sense of childhood would pale into insignificance here and I would learn silence.

I arrived on a Friday, and Friday's lunch was always mashed potato, peas and a fishfinger. However, on my first day, my first Friday, I was dished up an extra-large portion of fear. 'You're Not with the Babies Now' describes my introduction to the place I would call home for the remainder of my time as a child of the state system. I have tried to convey a sense of my abject fear and a hint of what was to come.

16. The Boy with the Broken Smile (page 67)

This is an evocative poem which gives a stunning description. Anyone who reads it will immediately have a vision of Paul as a young child. Paul talked to me a lot about what he described as his broken smile. He described himself as rarely smiling 'out loud', but in the last few years he had 'found his smile' as he describes in the video 'Labels are for tins not people'. Watch this to see Paul's words about finding his smile (and see some wonderful photos of him through his life).
(Siobhan)

17. Night Creeps In (page 68) and 18. Innocence Taken (page 71)

We have been unable to locate preambles for these poems. Many of the narratives of Paul's work come from when he read his work out at events and these two poems were rarely shared outside a small group of friends. What I notice is that in 'Night Creeps In' Paul uses the third person (he) and in 'Innocence Taken' he uses the first person (I). I know the stories behind these poems well, but I am conflicted about what to share. The poems do speak for themselves to some extent and perhaps don't need the detail of the stories. It is because of the experiences that Paul shares with us here that he began to watch out for others and become their protector. Something that he did throughout his life.
(Siobhan)

Sadly, the abuse Paul suffered wasn't only from the adults in his institutional life as, under the cover of darkness, older boys fulfilled their developing needs at the expense of the younger boys' innocence. Nobody protected Paul and his contemporaries from this additional trauma but, when Paul became one of the older boys, he tried to make sure those younger than himself did not suffer in the same way.
(Joanne)

19. Marks of an Unwanted Rainbow (page 72)

I've tried to convey the depth of a brutal system dished out to little children, and the physical and psychological impact of this on such small, vulnerable beings. A bruise is a bruise, eventually it fades, but bruising of the mind and heart doesn't disappear so easily and, in a lot of cases, never goes away; it's so much more than skin deep!

As a little boy, I learned to put up a front. I took what was dished out, believing I deserved it because, of course, it must have been my fault! It's not as if I had a choice really. I recall the number of times I hid myself away and sat quietly tracing outlines of marks, bruises and cuts on my skin. Inside I wept, but I would never let *them* see. It took me a lifetime to fully comprehend events that marked my childhood. Fostering children helped 'heal' my unseen bruises and I stopped blaming myself.

20. Sometimes I Stand Still (page 75)

Is it any wonder that the narratives that we have struggled to find relate to the poems which describe the abuse that Paul endured?

When Paul was reading his poems at events he liked to move. A lot! He also liked to read from the page. Paul told me that someone had told him that if he committed the poems to memory and "performed them more" they would have more impact on the audience, and he'd get more "bookings" (I'll keep it between us who told him that). Paul didn't want to commit the work to memory – he wanted to separate himself from what had happened, writing about his experiences had helped him to externalise what he had endured, and he needed to keep it there – on the pages or canvas.

He didn't want to stand still. He was moving ahead at speed when his life was so cruelly taken.
(Siobhan)

21. Hurtday (page 79)

This is a jointly written poem which was instigated by my wife, Sarah, following a conversation about my reluctance to celebrate or acknowledge my birthday. I explained how birthdays hold very little personal meaning for me as I and others weren't allowed to celebrate such occasions when we were children.

My first birthday celebration was my 18th. Some friends made me a cake, gave me a card, and took me to the 'Top Rank' in Birmingham. They even asked the DJ to play 'Jimmy Mac' for me!

I've reflected how, even as an adult, I struggle with marking my own birthday as it brings back so many memories and reminders of not being worthy even for 'one' day. I have always referred to it as a 'Hurtday' and just want it to pass as quickly as possible.

I do however make an effort for my children, my wife and friends. I want them to feel extra special for a day. It's the very least anyone deserves, and I am learning to accept some of the attention from those who love me on this date.

Thank you, Sarah, for helping me make sense of it all. xx

22. No Colours for My Coat (page 80)

People are very quick to judge and label what is in front of them. If we're honest, we all do and, of course, there are drawbacks with this process. As the old saying goes, 'mud sticks', and labels can become a 'destiny', a 'prediction', a 'prophecy'.

The names attributed to me and others I grew up with in care came at us without warning, from all directions, but were never asked for. The fact is they were relentless, and my tormentors came in many guises: Nuns, priests, teachers, parishioners, day-kids, Police, doctors, social workers, and foster carers. It felt like I was at the mercy of the world.

I wrote this poem to describe what it felt like for me, and how I coped. To begin to believe, and even subscribe to, the words people gave me felt like my own 'coat of labels', and yet I held some sort of notion that I might be all right. I believed that I wasn't all bad, but these thoughts remained private. I couldn't share them. I needed to have something that was mine.

I began to feel the need to create something to acknowledge this, so I started sewing labels on to an old jacket of mine. I cried a lot as I witnessed what was unfolding. It's hard to understand how I, as a little boy could be subjected to such words. Their intention to break me or destroy me seems pointless and meaningless, far beyond my comprehension!

But I am proud knowing that, not only did I survive their words, but I thrived. It took me a while, but I got there eventually.

23. A Moloch's Kiss (page 87)

Moloch: A biblical name of a Canaanite god associated with child sacrifice.

I recall the number of occasions that I was subjected to emotional and physical violence from the very people who were supposed to be looking after me. The rest of the world saw that these women and men had given up their lives for the benefit of others and, therefore, would compassionately love and nurture those less fortunate.

Being spat on made me feel so dirty and unwanted, the lowest of the low and so helpless because I couldn't do anything about it. The hurt I felt from being spat on was more painful than the blows because it felt like it crept inside me. For a while I believed this to be normal and felt that I actually deserved this kind of treatment.

Physical pain doesn't last, it's momentary and passes, but the words sealed by 'spit' travel deep within, impacting on emotional well-being and health.

I wrote this with the intention that it would conjure up the image of a small child being dragged by their hair, thrashed, beaten, feeling frightened, shaking, confused, scared and somehow trying to make sense of words screamed at him, and then dealing with the pain of being spat on! The fact is, I can still feel the kisses I received from a Moloch.

24. Have You Ever? (page 88)

Things happen. That's life, I guess, but growing up in care can feel so unfair.

Have you Ever is a personal and emotional portrayal of my childhood as I experienced it. I have tried to convey the feelings I felt and witnessed, things I was unable to speak about as a small boy and as a grown man. Tomorrow seemed so far away and came with the same promises as today, never offering respite.

I hope the reader senses the magnitude and, at times, desperation that engulfed me. I was awash with fear.

Yet, within me, a thread of belief existed, and I developed a resilience which occasionally searched for a glimpse of hope, the same hope that I perceived everyone else to have. It was this belief that enabled me to face each day, after all, I needed to believe in something.

25. Shadow Friend (page 92)

As a child 'shadow people' became mine. I felt safe with them because they never hurt me. They became a constant for me as they shared my life, my stories, my beatings, my abuse, my tears, and never once judged me, but always stayed loyal to me.

I spoke to my shadows. They became my friends. I told them about my fears, my sadness and my dreams because they knew how to keep secrets safe and would never 'grass'.

As a small boy, they somehow helped me make sense of the often chaotic world I was forced to grow up in. At times they even offered me a chance to smile when I made gestures in the sun.

26. White Boy (page 95)

Growing up in the 1960s and 70s, the vast majority of children in the children's home were mixed race and covered a variety of different shades.

Society, let alone the religious institution I grew up in, were neither accepting nor tolerant of our arrival. We therefore experienced the ugly side of humankind and, from as early as I can remember, I was taught to feel ashamed because I was 'coloured'. This only added to the feelings of not being good enough and the need to be subservient to 'white' people.

I didn't understand that I was 'coloured' (that hadn't been explained to me) except for the names I was called and, like the majority, I wanted to be seen as white. Positive black (the generic reference to us all) role models were in short supply and rarely, if at all, referred to. Our exposure was limited to references to slavery or films like Tarzan and Carry on Up the Khyber/Jungle. We could aspire to be porters or savages, not much of a choice!

White boy was a nickname used for one of my 'brothers' who articulated how many of us saw ourselves. None of us wanted to believe we were bad just because of our tone of skin. For him and many others, discovery of our 'blackness' was self-taught, and there have been real struggles for some to come to terms with their mixed ethnicity. Personally, seeing ethnicity as something positive strengthens the foundations of my identity and helps me to be proud of who I am.

27. Number 10 (page 96)

In the children's home the children were assigned a number. Paul was number 10.

Through the time that I knew Paul, he returned to his given name Yusuf. This name was taken away from him by the nuns who instead gave him the name Paul. Most of the time, though, the nuns referred to this wonderful little boy as "10." The amazing piece of artwork 'No colours for my coat' has the number 10 sewn in as a name label.

Paul did not consistently use the name Yusuf. He told me he was experimenting with using it and felt more comfortable using it as a 'professional' identity. To some people Paul was Paul, to others he was Yusuf. After leaving the children's

home he was never again number 10, yet when he set up his website, he gave it the name www.pyusuf10.com to recognise the three 'names' he had.
(Siobhan)

28. What Are You Then? (page 99)

Even today, when I think back and remember how adults spoke to me, it sends shivers through my body. The dismissive language applied was another way of keeping me and others down. Their assumptions about me, so freely announced, had little regard to the degradation they inflicted.

To be told that, "Children like you are wrong...just wrong", stripped away any self-esteem I might have had.

29. 'Cos I Care (page 100)

As a small boy I was referred to as 'someone' who was sullen, troubled and certainly incapable of being good. They had lots of negative words for me, and I often felt I was some sort of target for others to vent their hatred.

It's a difficult burden to carry, knowing you weren't well thought of, especially when so small.

I discovered that I could hide away for ages (something I was extremely good at) and no one really looked for me, but it also made me sad to feel that no one cared enough to even try.

I loved nature and natural things. I was able to touch things without being hurt, and it allowed me to escape from my daily madness. I believed that if I spoke with or touched nature, I would be able to change my life (I sometimes screwed my eyes so tight and *really, really* prayed that this would happen). I was able to ask the questions I wanted to, and I hoped I'd get some answers. I just needed to believe that someone was on my side, so to speak.

'Cos I Care captures me visually as I make attempts to acknowledge my own worth, using the limited world around me. Care is a lonely place to be in, especially when you realise that not all is right with the world, but you just don't know why. All you understand is that you don't feel happy inside.

I still wanted, or rather needed, to know that someone could care apart from me. Feeling that I was believed or heard by 'someone' fuelled my hope.

30. Just Once (page 104)

Just Once is a short reflective piece that I hope gives some insight into the confusion and feelings of loss and isolation I felt. I have tried to find words and expressions that I couldn't articulate as a small boy. This was written with tears as it reminded me of the desolation and loneliness I felt as a little boy trying desperately to cope with all that was going on, fearful, mistrustful, a boy who needed to know that someone cared about him.

31. Rooster Boy (page 107)

I sometimes think about the many people I grew up with and, sadly, several are no longer with us, having taken decisions to disappear for ever. The sad fact is that many of those who successfully ended their lives did so because of the childhood traumas gifted to them by a regime that should never have been allowed to look after children. To be told your mother was nothing more than a prostitute and, by default, you were the lowest of the low is hard to take at any point, but when you're impressionable or looking to adults to help you gain an understanding of who you are, it's inexcusable. To be raised to believe you're not good enough and that you are despised is inhuman.

As a group, every loss of a 'brother' is felt. We are fortunate to have known them as the child they were before they became the person shaped by their time in state care. What saddens me is to hear the rhetoric and nonsense pontificated by those who were in charge and could have done things differently. Even today, they refuse to acknowledge that they were in any way culpable.

32. Foster Kid (page 108)

I wrote this when I thought about the options, or rather the lack of options, offered to me during my time in care. I seemed to be surrounded by people who allegedly had my best intentions at the forefront of their minds, yet they consistently ignored my feelings, my needs, and my wants. They chose to ignore signs of the treatment I endured which were evident in my demeanour. Their notes stated, 'He's happy with his lot'.

Another new face would appear, my story would be regurgitated, my background laid bare, and I was expected to co-operate.

Eventually, I closed my eyes and ears to their requests, to their decisions. I no longer wanted any part of their 'system', just to be left alone where I could take time to figure out my life.

Today it still feels like these experiences continue. Very little choice is on offer, and children like me who never chose their circumstances still go through the system as if on some production line. Little regard to additional loss and separation is acknowledged, and the constant need to regurgitate the child's narrative (mainly the negative aspects) goes on and, like me, their story becomes unimportant.

33. The Expert on Floors and Halls (page 111)

Foster care for me was all rather strange, almost beyond me. Except for one family who I maintained a degree of contact with, I found the whole experience damaging to me. Lack of consultation probably fed this. My longest consecutive period was a six-week school holiday, and the shortest was one day, with a mixture in between. In my mind I believed that I wasn't really wanted, just a child to help these people feel better about themselves: 'You're so good giving a child a taste of a family'! Eventually, I resolved in my mind that all episodes of foster care would be short; I would make them get rid of me.

The Expert on Floors and Halls refers to the many homes I went into. Conversations would be held about me as if I wasn't there. I noticed the differences, the people, the stares, the requests and demands made of me even before my bag had touched the floor. I liked to touch the walls, it reminded me that it was real, that it was happening.

34. Stolen Tears (page 112)

In that first rush of tears, I wrote this as I recalled my own vow never to cry again. I would have been barely six years of age. To believe that my tears were wasted, that any expression of sorrow or deep feelings I had would be ignored, punished, ridiculed and never heard, helped me as I found the strength to shut down and not let people see how hurt I felt inside.

Physical abuse is difficult to receive, but it was the emotional abuse that stung me far deeper and was painfully at odds with my core belief that kindness should be something everyone can receive, even me. I look back as an adult and refer to this release of tears as stolen tears that I couldn't express during my early childhood.

35. A Stranger Who Knew (page 115)

Not too long ago I had the opportunity to meet up with a very diverse group of people who had grown up in the care system. We talked and acknowledged that, despite not knowing each other before, there was a kind of understanding and respect, perhaps best described as a 'natural' connection.

I was asked to read some pieces of my writing. Whilst reading, a couple of individuals left the room and approached me later, firstly to apologise for walking out, but also to explain that listening to my words felt like I was telling their story. They asked for another reading, and we all shared some tears regarding our experiences. They thanked me for giving words to their pain, for naming their emotions and for giving them permission to feel what they felt. I was privileged to have this level of disclosure and honesty offered to me, and so I wrote this poem as an acknowledgment of their words about me. I was humbled that my words, my story helped them.

I hope it gives them some peace and I dedicate this to us all.

36. I Cried Today (page 116)

In November 2015, I finally found courage to put into words the feelings and experiences I had as a child growing up in a children's home. I wrote a piece, a short verse called 'A Butterflies Heartbeat' to describe how I coped following a brutal beating at the hands of my nemesis when I was approximately 5 years of age. As I started to read it aloud tears started to form. I couldn't read further and, unexpectedly, I let out a wail and tears flowed. I couldn't stop. I hadn't cried since I was six years of age. I cried and I cried for the little boy who I once was and whose childhood had been taken from me by the people who should have cared for me.

37. Let it All Go (page 119)

Unbeknown to me, all my demons and torment came to the surface and, like a man possessed, I started to write and write and write. I couldn't and still can't stop; for me it became important to tell my story and to voice, on behalf of others, the wrongs of our experiences. Perhaps more importantly I hoped to give voice to the emotional mindset a child like me experienced growing up. I hoped that those in charge or who have the wherewithal to make positive changes and improve outcomes for 'looked after children' would take note and hopefully gain some insight into how it feels to be growing up in a system that isn't always geared up to nurture and support the very children it is designed for!!

38. I Can Dream at Night (page 120)

Someone commented on how well I was looking, that I no longer looked so tired. I smiled and replied, "I sleep now, I even get to dream".

Through most of my childhood and adulthood I survived on minimal hours of sleep. I was afraid of tormentors, visitors in the night, those who came to hurt me. This fear evolved into nightmares and wakeful nights and even in the daytime I remained alert. I was even fearful at times of my own shadow.

Since writing I have been able to remove the weight I carried on my shoulders. Allowing myself to cry, mourn, to get angry, shout, rant and hear my voice verbalise what happened to me has helped me find my inner sanctum where peace resides. It has also banished my nightmares, and I now sleep well. I finally get to dream with a smile.

39. This Boy is Always in Trouble (page 123)

I took charge of my 'care' file in my mid-thirties. My expectations weren't too high. I'd hoped that there would be at least basic information or recordings of my childhood milestones, the little stuff I knew nothing about. I guess I hoped that there might be information that would prove my birth family cared. I was, therefore, surprised to receive a file that was only 12mm thick (8mm after some school reports were removed!); not much considering I'd spent eighteen years as a child of the state.

Nevertheless, I turned the sheets of paper. It felt at first glance that someone had hastily put the file together and, at worst, with a degree of contempt. Did they still hold contempt for me and the others that had the misfortune to have grown up here?! Sheets of a childhood, in no order, making little sense; ironically a true reflection of my childhood. Later, once I put everything in date order, I began the process of learning about me and why I'd become a child of the state system.

A little was written of my growing up in Pallotti, details of walking, talking, and even reference to my first real 'friend'...Jumbo (He disappeared when I arrived in Coleshill as they took him away, screaming at me that 'toys are for babies'). There was nothing from when I first arrived at St Edwards until aged eleven. No records or notation of anything that happened to me as a little boy, nothing...except the entry on a medical sheet, "This boy is always in trouble". I tried to discover what this 'ailment' meant but, alas, I had to accept that I was a unique medical marvel as I appear to be the only child who suffered with this condition.

40. Did I Like Balloons? (page 124)

Having a sense of who you are is important, knowing bits about yourself is too. It helps to create aspects of identity that can tell you that you belong. As a dad, I'm able to offer my children anecdotes and stories of their earlier life, confirming their memories and giving them a sense of time. They still like to hear stories about their early childhood, and that's a good thing as it helps them understand how they belong to our family.

For a child like me, growing up in institutions, I had to rely on my own memory, which is so much harder. I still remember being coerced into entering a 'guess the baby competition' in my first employment. Part of the competition involved guessing birth weight, and age of talking and walking. Everyone else had pictures of themselves as a baby; all I had was a picture of me lined up with a group of children surrounded by nuns. If I showed it, everyone would know part of my story, and would no doubt ask questions which I didn't have the answers to. I didn't want people to pity me, and eventually dropped out of the competition, giving some sort of excuse. They all thought I was a little weird anyway, so there was no change there!

Receiving my file in my mid-thirties enabled me to at least get some basic information about my childhood.

41. Look at Me Now (page 127)

I love this one! it feels angry, it feels loud, it feels right, it feels justified, it feels 'in your face'.

I wrote it not long after I learned to cry. I felt good about myself. I recognised and felt the love my family had for me without any judgement. I finally 'got it', that I was worthy, I was always worthy, and so I wanted to shout at those who turned away, who should have cared for me and all the others. I wanted them to understand that, despite their cavalier attitude and contempt that they still hold for me and others who grew up in their 'care', I and so many others have achieved and are loved.

42. Going Back (page 128)

For a brief period of years, I became a 'panel' member for an independent fostering agency, an agency that had links to the place I grew up in. My rationale for this has never changed: Every child matters.

I saw my involvement as an opportunity in part to redress the lack of accountability that was afforded for children like me. My role was to ensure that the voice of the child was central to any panel decisions. However, I underestimated the feelings that were stirred each time I entered the grounds of my childhood; so many frightening memories, so many lost faces who never made it through.

I forced myself to 'go in'. I needed to believe that, given my time again, someone would have stepped up to ensure my rights and needs would be protected. So I attended the panel.

43. Our Dilemma (page 131)

Throughout my childhood, I and others were made to believe that we deserved the treatment that was dished out to us, and that we should be "grateful". Those words were used a lot to justify the actions of our abusers.

During my childhood I tried to protect those that were smaller and more vulnerable than me, children who needed a bit more time. Somehow, I felt responsible, I'm not sure why. Usually this was to my detriment, but if I could deflect the beating, abuse or anger being projected at them, then that was enough. I had already decided that I didn't matter anyway, so what else could they do to hurt me more!

I still question whether I could have done more to prevent events occurring, to take on more of the burden, but sometimes I just didn't have the strength or courage. It's even harder knowing that some of my 'brothers' out there are still petrified, that they still have nightmares, and their daily lives continue to be affected by those childhood experiences, impacting on their mental health and well-being.

44. Despicable Me, Despicable You (page 132)

I wrote this with a view to giving an insight into me growing up in institutional care. Born into care, the first four years, though regimental, were at the very least more conducive and, dare I say, littered with pockets of happiness. Aged four and a half, I was transferred from one end of the country to the other. With a mixture of excitement and trepidation, I entered a new arena oblivious to the fact that any semblance of childhood I had was about to be removed. Abuse on every level would now take its place beside me.

To know that you're not good enough is hard to swallow but knowing that you're not wanted on any level, or that you can't be loved, eats away emotionally, and is devastating when you're so small. The emotional abuse in the form of words stung me the most. Physical abuse, though unpleasant, was momentary for me. The words spoken, on the other hand, were a lot for me to grasp and make sense of. I think, because of the spiteful manner in which they were delivered, I understood that the words were meant and laced with hatred and venom.

Despite this I somehow believed that I wasn't everything they said. I called it 'my hope', and I was always ready to forgive them in exchange for a piece of kindness. I didn't want much, just a little bit to keep me going. This poem aims to play back the orchestra of words (and their intent) that were hurled at me. I had no choice but to stand still. Fear and silence had already taught me that so, rooted to the spot I, endured the 'colourful' language of the kaleidoscope that reflects my life.

45. I Am (page 135)

There is a strength to this poem which reflects Paul's growing self-belief and understanding. It is a succinct message to the perpetrators of his abuse that he weathered the storm and remembers everything.
(Joanne)

46. Politician, Politician (page 136)

This one's a bit of a rant. I watch the news, read articles, view social media and I'm filled with a bad taste in my mouth by the nonsense I hear. Not only do I find it inhumane, but I find it uncaring and callous that money is put before the welfare of children who didn't get the 'rub of the green'. Lies are spouted to acquire votes, and I still witness the fear, the disdain that is applied to 'looked after' children who ultimately never chose their path. My ask is simple, treat us like your own, it's the very least we deserve.

47. Forgotten Promises (page 139)

As a small boy I clung on to some mistaken belief that I was being tested by being in the harsh environment of a children's home. I believed for a while that once I passed this test my family would come to collect me and, like all fairy stories, a happy ending would be mine. Unfortunately, this wasn't the case for me or most of us there.

In my mid-twenties I eventually met my birth mother. She told me at the first meeting how she had wanted to keep me but felt unable to do so: "I remember whispering to you that I'd find a way to get you back." She also said that she nearly came up once but was worried what people may have thought.

Comments like, "I never forgot you", were small comforts I suppose, and I took away that she at least had given some thought to me over the years. We all need to believe that someone out there cares.

In my mid-thirties, when I obtained my file, I read a couple of letters my birth mother had written. It seemed she was a frightened woman who *had* cared and, reading between the lines, seemed to have wanted to come back and take me with her, providing I wasn't noticed as coloured (her words and her greatest fear).

Forgotten Promises reflects a child who waited, who believed and who clung on to his misconception that someone was coming back for him.

48. Meeting Mother (page 140)

I often thought about my mother when I was small. She became a fantasy of my imagination. Unfortunately, I struggled to hold a picture of her inside my mind's eye. When I saw women outside the grounds of the children's home, I often wondered if that's what she looked like. I hoped she would have a softness about her and have hands that were gentle. I spoke to her a lot in my head, asking all manner of questions which all led back to why she didn't want me. What had I done that was so bad? It was difficult not knowing why I was in care, combined with the daily messages of distaste offered by those who were in charge.

49. The Other Me (page 143)

Identity is something we all cling onto and hold dear to ourselves. It starts with your name, your ethnicity, your culture and evolves and grows with you, becoming part of you, becoming you. Children coming into care usually have only their name that belongs to them, so to remove that too, is to strip away every aspect of who they are. The rationale applied may actually be with good intentions, but it still remains that the child is no longer whole.

Quite late in my adulthood I had feelings and thoughts resurrected following a conversation with my mother. I was reminded by others who I had grown up with that we were uncomfortable with our given names. My suspicions about why my name was chosen were not totally unfounded, but to find out it was never given by my mother, rather chosen by an organisation that didn't care, was a final insult. Had I known, maybe I would have had a clearer sense of who I was from an earlier age.

50. A Mother's Blessing... Not Me (page 144)

I've known of my birth family for some years now and have had plenty of time to consider all the factors of me being placed into care. That has never been much of an issue, as I do understand that the climate was somewhat different when I arrived in the world than it is today. What I've also come to understand is the importance of relationships and, despite being related biologically, it doesn't mean that connections are there. My relationship with my mother has always been civil; conversations have never been very deep or meaningful. Unfortunately, despite offering my forgiveness and apportioning no blame, my birth mother is unable to rid herself of her own guilt and, therefore, has been unable to forgive herself which has meant our relationship has failed to progress or develop.

A Mother's Blessing is my way of explaining how it feels and the impact it has on me, all of which my mother has refused to hear. It saddens me as she has missed out on my wonderful children and the possibilities of a son.

51. My Feelings Tread So Softly (page 151)

Paul's relationship with his mother was an artificial, shallow affair, where she never publicly acknowledged that he was her son. He never received any straight answers regarding his background nor any apology nor heartfelt enquiry after his feelings. She had difficulty remembering his children's names. He could not share his experiences with her as she would not believe what he said. He gave up attempting to discuss his childhood, treading softly around her for her sake.
(Sarah)

52. I Am Worthy (page 152)

The fact that this is the fifty-second poem in this work is no mistake, because it was at the age of fifty-two when Paul finally came to terms with his past and began to make sense of the significant events of his childhood. This short poem is the culmination of all that has gone before as described in the previous poems. The poems have been ordered as far as possible to depict Paul's turbulent journey through life. I Am Worthy is a short, but very important, piece that shows, despite all the hardship, Paul's golden thread of belief eventually brought him to a place where he could acknowledge his own worth.
(Joanne)

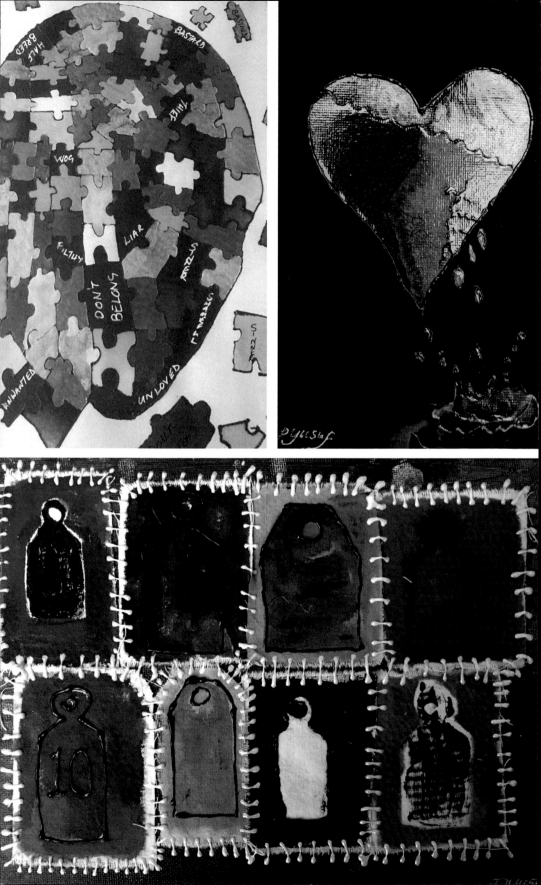

The Final 'Article'

There is both an irony and a huge sadness that the final thing that Paul wrote was about Covid, the terrible virus that robbed us all of this wonderful man. In the abusive institutions where Paul grew up the nuns often called him a 'dirty article' (it appears on the labels of his coat) and so he never liked to talk about articles, only 'pieces' that he had written. This is the final piece that Paul wrote. It shows that even in the midst of a terrifying pandemic he was thinking of the impact on children and what he could do to make their lives better. That was Paul Yusuf McCormack.

Covid-19 and fostering: Can we learn and take the creative approaches being used to continue doing things differently for our looked after children?

Like the rest of the world Covid-19 has changed our landscape and the impact has been felt globally. Closer to home paid work for me ceased, schools and colleges closed, Artifacts, my newly set up business put on hold and as a family we're no longer able to see our older children or close friends. We're supporting home schooling for our youngest two whilst also fostering two unrelated children with very different needs. The only thing not to dry up is my artwork, and when you're impatient to crack on, it can be a bit of a tough gig.

However, I'd like to speak about fostering during these unusual times. We're looking after two children, one a toddler who has just accomplished the art of walking and thus is creating merry havoc as he can get into even more mischief. The other is an older child with much more complexity and unknowns, who has little confidence, very low self-esteem, hasn't engaged or been involved with education and believes everything around them will either kill or poison them.

All the children's social workers operate differently, one still comes to see their child, the other speaks via a video link. A positive result of Covid-19, has been that a technical dinosaur like me has learned to set up and operate Zoom, Skype & Microsoft Teams! Our own support social worker operates via text or telephone. Bearing in mind all three social workers operate from the same authority, it sends out conflicting and confusing messages as they all have interpreted 'social distancing' differently. As adults we can deal with these frustrations but imagine how it may feel from a child's perspective.

Foster carers, like most parents in the country, are feeling the strain of managing children of varying ages and needs at home every day. We all agree that children, perhaps more so than adults, need structure and routine to their days and weeks and maintaining old routines at this current time feels like a juggling act. For all our children the landscape has changed so that school, breakfast and after-school clubs, sports, parties or simply playing with friends now look very different. As foster carers we are having to take on new roles including managing, overseeing and supporting all schoolwork sent from schools. For many of us and our children this maintains routines and learning, but for some carers it will undoubtedly be a great source of tension and stress in the home.

The most striking challenge faced by our children, their families and us as foster carers at this time of Covid-19 crisis is the disruption caused to the child's ability to maintain contact with their family. Many family time arrangements have been severely disrupted or ceased because of the crisis. In the beginning of the crisis, when initial measures such as recommendations for 'social distancing' and reducing contact with vulnerable people were made, many foster carers expressed concern about how these measures were incompatible with existing contact arrangements. Some of us raised concerns around having people with underlying health conditions within the family home and how a child maintaining a previously existing contact arrangement put those vulnerable people at increased risk of contracting Covid-19. In some cases, members of the children's family are working in healthcare settings and we expressed concern around these individuals carrying the virus and transferring it during contact. We understand that social workers and their managers assess each case individually to assess the reasonableness of the concerns, the potential impact on the child of a disruption in contact and the alternative means of maintaining some form of contact. However, it can feel that in this scenario that while all professionals are equal, and their voices are considered, some professionals are more equal than others!

As foster carers we recognise and support the child's right to remain connected to their families and we know that this is supported and encouraged by social workers. I think we all 'get' the need to help rebuild interrupted relationships between children and their birth family so even for someone like me, a technical dinosaur, we have had to look creatively at how we can remain engaged and support our children. Due to the different needs and ages of our children we have instigated mini-video clips of our younger child, who wouldn't be able to gain anything meaningful from a video chat. We have also suggested their family videos themselves reading a bedtime story which we could play back. We already know from the messages we receive from their birth family how seeing such footage has reassured them.

Our older child has weekly video

chats and we have encouraged their parents to become involved in reading during these chats. We copy the pages to read and send across to parents and exchange letters and pictures. Again, it offers reassurance from the child's perspective as they can see their parents are okay, it allows the parents to be actively involved too. Our child also gets to speak with their older adult siblings, again this helps to preserve and strengthen that part of a child's identity.

The disruption and distress caused by the Covid-19 crisis for children in care, presents both the children and the caring adults in their lives with new opportunities to explore methods of staying connected that may previously have been unexplored. As foster carers we do sometimes have valid reasons and concerns around maintaining appropriate boundaries with birth parents and do not wish to give parents our personal phone details or social media platform details. This shouldn't be viewed negatively; it presents an opportunity to work more creatively. A free SIM card could be topped up to enable WhatsApp to be deployed and allow texting, small video clips and voice messaging. Social workers could work with foster cares to develop appropriate boundaries, whilst still monitoring and satisfying themselves with regards to the child's well- being and experience.

For some children using video contact could be a positive safe form of 'family time' as it may provide an experience which is not n as emotionally charged, or as intense an experience for the child, as a face-to-face meeting can be. It may be a method which potentially serves towards building a structure that works better for the child.

As foster carers I would expect us to be best placed to judge how the child reacts and responds to this form of communication. We should monitor our children's baseline behaviour and presentation against their behaviour in the lead up, during and after the video contact. We have had to recognise that, for our older child, their anxiety levels and certainly the number of questions increase as does the level of 'fidgeting'. We know the signs when the restlessness means time for the call to end and we have to step in, allowing our child to leave the room and we will finish off the conversations, usually filling in some of the gaps that they haven't mentioned. Fortunately, the rapport we have built with our children's parents is positive and we can share concerns and alleviate some of their worries. Success will always look different due to the uniqueness of our children and will depend on several factors. Different children have differing interests and temperaments and engage to varying degrees. Trying to understand the nature of the relationship and attachment the child had with their parent/family prior to coming into care is crucial especially if the child is having to adapt to a previously unexplored or used method of communication. Just talking face to face for any length of time may be a whole new experience.

Our youngest is blissfully unaware what all the fuss is about. Every day they get to eat, play, experience and explore the world around them and deservingly relish being spoilt with lots of cuddles and hugs, plus they still get to see their birth family twice a week...what is there not to like about that.

On the other hand, Covid-19 has increased our older child's anxieties and worries. This means an increase in questions. They are conscious of the current situation and struggle with their anxieties even more, as it has increased their additional worries about their birth family, teachers, us, even our cat. Maintaining routines, wherever possible, has been the way forward. School hours have been reduced. They continue to attend, so as to maintain a level of structure, which is important as they had been out of school since 2019.

Typically, each day is full of questions. They start first thing in the morning and can be quite random such as "If I use body wash will that kill off bacteria?" "Can the cat catch it?" "Will the virus land on my curtains if I leave the window open?" to "I heard more children in care will die, will I be dying soon?", and "Can it land on tyres and live on roads and pavements?"

We don't have all the answers but try to offer reassurance by talking through each scenario to try and get understanding of where they are coming from. It can be tiresome but it's clearly important. Every morning they insist on watching the news (national, as local news would be too close to home) which means we can discuss and address some of their concerns, and that's even before they start the school journey.

"Will they have wiped the taxi down when it comes to collect me?" "Will the driver be wearing a mask?" "Will the teachers pass the disease to me?" We try and talk through each one getting the young person to draw out the most rational response. It satisfies them until the next day and we play out the same ritual again. Fresh towel and bacterial soap is packed so they don't have to share with anyone else, and off they go.

On return, clothes are put for washing, a shower or good wash is taken and we have a hot drink discussing how the day has been. Conversation then centres around family, why can't I go back and when can I see them again? Due to the current situation physical contact with birth family is every three weeks. In between as I've already highlighted we've arranged video weekly chats. For this particular child they struggle with the idea that the younger child still gets family time twice a week and they can only see their family for two hours every three weeks. We agree that it doesn't feel fair, especially when both children are under the same Local Authority. Naturally we have raised these concerns and issues, seeking a degree of reassurance, whilst trying to be supportive of our children.

I think we all have learned to do things differently and creatively. I feel it has meant a much more child-centred approach. That has to be a good thing! The Covid-19 crisis continues to be an unprecedented event in our lifetime. Social workers haven't had time to prepare strategies around keeping children safe to the greatest degree possible, whilst minimising the upset and disruption caused to the children we all work with. What I believe is it highlights the importance of relationships. It is important that social workers become a significant person in the child's life. Recognising that this may have been a frightening and confusing time for many children in care, means acknowledging they will be ever-more reliant on the safe, familiar and consistent people in their lives to guide them through it.

Decisions made in relation to the child's lived experience of this time may have effects that will last well beyond Covid-19. The type of communication and relationship the child is able to have with the most significant people in their lives is therefore of crucial importance. Social workers need to proactively and creatively protect the relationships the child has and incorporate the maintenance of these relationships in to the strategies for guiding and supporting the child through this crisis. As always, the child's welfare must be placed at the centre of all we do, and the role of the social worker is to manage, support and encourage all to work towards what is best for the child. These principles apply generally to all aspects of the life of a child in care, but are acutely highlighted at this time of unprecedented and unpredictable challenges.

Yusuf P McCormack

I WILL
CHOOSE
WHO I
WANT
TO BE

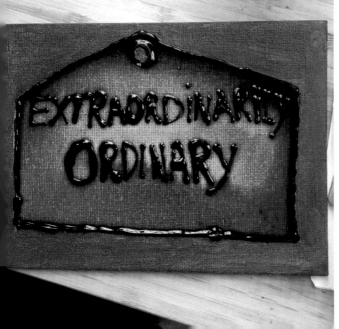

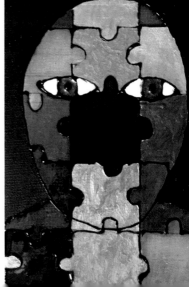

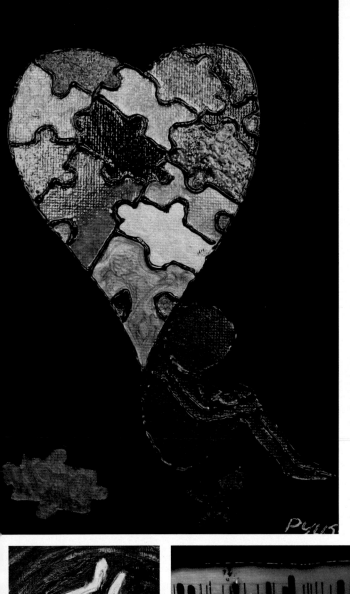

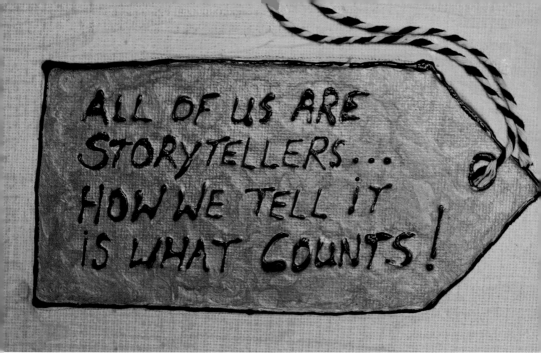

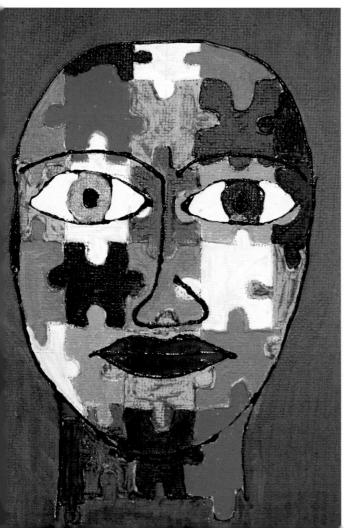

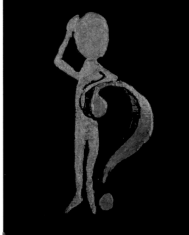

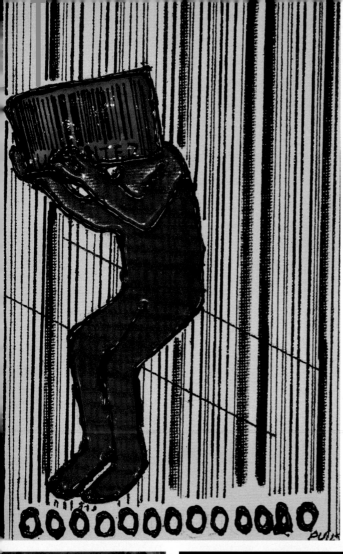

Using this Book as a Social Work Learning Tool

Siobhan Maclean

Paul produced reams of poems and verse. He found the creative process cathartic, but he wanted his work to go beyond this. Paul wanted to refine his poetry for publication and more than anything he wanted them to be useful for social work education. Paul was one of the people most committed to improving social work education that I have ever met. He continually asked social workers to stop talking about wanting to make a difference and simply start BEING the difference. He was a brilliant teacher and guide to social work students, and often engaged in personal communication with students to support them along their journey.

We agreed therefore that there should be 52 poems in this book, for two reasons. Paul first started to write about his experiences at age 52, as he shares in the preface, and there are 52 weeks in the year. Paul wanted social work students and educators to think about a different poem and piece of artwork each week for a year. In this way he hoped that reading the poem and considering the art would become part of a slowed down reflective process. We both loved the verse:

> "If you listen slow
> Some of what I say
> Will enter your heart"
> (Unknown in Maclean, Finch and Tedam 2018)

This book should be used 'slowly' in a range of ways. Take your time with it to find new ways to explore Paul's experiences and perspectives. The following ideas are just that – ideas. You will find your own way to use the book.

University lecturers: Put the book on reading lists. Include the voice of Paul Yusuf McCormack in all your teaching. This book crosses a wide range of modules and can be used to support learning across the whole social work professional curriculum.

Practice educators and supervisors: Make space for the book in your supervision sessions. Use it as a discussion point. Pull out specific tasks. This will help students to develop their skills in a range of areas.

Students: Visit this book regularly. Take with you the central message that you can BE the difference. Ask yourself "How can I be the difference?" in every situation you encounter.

Social workers: Use this book as part of your CPD. Reflect on the poetry and the art and the messages that you see. How can you be the difference in everything that you do?

Social work trainers: Paul's work has a great deal to offer in training on a variety of topics. Some of the following suggested activities work well as part of a training course.

Visual thinking: Traditionally, social work education and training has placed a strong emphasis on thinking verbally often at the expense of visual skills. I have used visual thinking in my work for some time and this has been questioned on occasions, particularly by academics who seem to feel that visual thinking techniques can undermine the importance of analytical thought. However, maths and science are increasingly using visual techniques, specifically in analysis, and visual thinking has been particularly valuable in the development of complexity theory (Johnson 2011) which has a great deal to offer contemporary social work.

The business world is increasingly using visual thinking strategies, with research indicating that this has enabled businesses to:

- Manage complex organisational problems
- Break down silos
- Empower staff teams and individuals to create, and build on, new ideas
- Foster collaborative practice
- Promote co-creation

(Brand, Koene and Ars 2017)

Research in organisational practice has also reported that visual thinking is particularly helpful in relation to decision-making, identifying that it can help in reaching 'better decisions faster' and in communicating decisions to others more effectively (Roam 2009). So, there could well be a number of benefits to using visual thinking in practice, particularly in helping students to develop key skills around analysis and dealing with complexity in practice. There has been substantially more research in nursing than social work about the use of visual thinking in eduaction. For example, Moorman (2017) suggests that the use of visual thinking techniques with nursing students supports the development of observational skills and critical thinking.

Using art to develop analytical skills in groups: Art, much like life, can very often be understood on a range of levels which is perhaps why it can be so useful in developing analytical skills. There is a growing body of research around the use of art appreciation to develop analysis (Pellico et al 2005, Ostafin and Kassman 2012, Fook et al 2016). The following activity is generally best done in a small group, although it can be carried out on a one-to-one basis too. Show the group participants the same piece of artwork and ask them:

- What do you see?
- What do you think Paul Yusuf McCormack was trying to communicate?

Following this discussion ask people to think about:

- What didn't you see that others saw?
- Why didn't you see that?

Discussions about what people didn't see are often the most enlightening, and this is where discussions about conformational bias or attributional bias can be brought out. Quickly people recognise that they are seeing the same thing but that they are interpreting it differently. This can lead to interesting discussions about the way that two social workers can visit the same family and see their situation very differently. Why is that? How can we address that in decision-making processes? All of these are interesting discussion points to draw out. There is a famous quote, attributed to American psychologist Wayne Dyer "Change the way you see things and the things you see change." This can be useful to add to discussions around what people see in the art.

Look beyond the 'obvious': When I have discussed Paul's work with students, I often hear them use the word obvious ("*Obviously the picture is a person and…*"). It is only obvious to you! Look beyond what you see. Look at a piece of artwork and make a brief note about what you see. Look again a week or so later. Now what do you see? A month later and you will see something else. Why?

Use the 'What? Why? How?' framework
Use the What? Why? How? framework to think through things like:

- What do I see in this artwork?
- Why?
- How might this impact on me and my work?

Talk to your colleagues about the artwork:

- What do they see?
- Why does that differ to what you see?
- How might the different things that you each see be helpful to one another?

Talk to others / discuss the book: Social workers should be clear that silence harms. In fact, silence can kill. For example, we know that in terms of racism, white silence is hugely harmful. It is vital that we talk about what has happened in care systems so that we can make sure that it doesn't continue to happen. Talk about this book. Talk about your reflections. Talk about the experiences of Paul Yusuf McCormack. Talk.

Write a poem or create some art in response: Creativity is vital in social work. We need to be able to use creative approaches in our work. Try out developing a creative response to this text. Write a poem or develop some artwork – or both! Use your creativity however you want to.

Find a word: This can be useful for verbal thinkers. Find a word that describes the art you see. A single word. Paul didn't title all his pieces and he described himself as "not precious about titles". What word would you use to title each piece of art. Why?

If you had to find a single word to sum up your experience of reading this book what would it be?

Reconsider 'titles': I have said a number of times that Paul did not generally feel strongly about titles, but he was very definite about the title of this book. Why might that have been? On page 17 I said that I may not have chosen the same title. Why might I say that? Would you have selected a different title? What would it be? Why?

Explore themes: On pages 10-15 I explore what I see as some of the key themes to Paul's artwork. It is common to hear people talking about 'emerging themes' in research but really they emerge because of the researcher and the way that they see the information they have gathered. What themes do you see in Paul's work? (Either the poems or the artwork). Why do those themes emerge for you?

Think about social work theory: Paul was really interested in social work theory and how it connected to practice. He found understanding the thinking behind particular approaches interesting and would often make references to theory in his speaking. What theories can you see in the artwork included in this text? Why do you see those?

Reflective tasks: Whilst reflecting on individual poems and art is important, then there are also some general reflective tasks that you could explore as part of using this book.

- Think about the positioning of the artwork. A great deal of thought went into what went where and many conversations took place around this. What messages do you see in the positioning of the art? For example, think about the size of the pictures. What might the messages in this be? How might the pictures, which have been used, connect together and 'grow' initial messages?

- Some of the poems don't have a specific piece of art attached, but there are lots of pieces of art elsewhere in the book. What art would you have included instead of the photographs? Why? How might that have altered the readers experience?

References

Brand, W., Koene, P. and Ars, M. (2017) Visual Thinking: Empowering people and organisations through visual collaboration. (London) Laurence King Publishing.

Fook, J., Collington, V., Ross, F., Ruch, G. and West, L. (Eds) (2016) Researching Critical Reflection: Multi-disciplinary Perspectives. (Oxon) Routledge

Johnson, N. (2011) Simply Complexity: A Clear Guide to Complexity Theory. (Oxford) Oneworld Publications.

Maclean, S., Finch, J. and Tedam, P. (2018) SHARE: A New Model for Social Work. (Lichfield) Kirwin Maclean Associates.

Moorman, M. (2017) The Use of Visual Thinking Strategies and Art to Help Nurses Find Their Voices. Creative Nursing 23 (3) 167-171. Doi. 10.1891/1078- 4535.23.3.167

Ostafin, B.D. and Kassman, K.T. (2012) Stepping out of history: Mindfulness improves insight problem solving. Consciousness and Cognition 21 (2) 1031- 1036.

Pellico, L.H., Friedlaender, and L., Fennie, K.P, (2005) Looking is not Seeing: Using Art to Improve Observational Skills. Journal of Nurse Education, 8 (11) 648-653

Roam, D. (2009) Unfolding the Napkin: The Hands-On Method for Solving Complex Problems with Simple Pictures. (New York) Portfolio Press

Exploring the body of Paul / Yusuf's work

 Instagram page can be found at
https://www.instagram.com/p.yusuf10/

 Yusuf was a member of the organising committee
for the Care Experienced Conference, the report of
which can be found at: https://docs.wixstatic.com/
ugd/7773fa_408ccafe514e4f0193e4dfbdb2637808.pdf

 A selection of interviews which Yusuf did can be viewed at the
following: https://issuu.com/socialworknews/docs/swn_jan-
mar_190128/10

 Yusuf Paul McCormack: 'I would have loved somebody older
to have said – you're going to be OK' | Child protection | The
Guardian

 https://soundcloud.com/user-724872833/care-to-listen-p-yusuf-
mccormack-what-did-you-do-wrong-to-be-in-care

 https://www.buzzsprout.com/1275323/5452552-part-1-insights-
into-two-care-leavers-education-experience

 https://www.buzzsprout.com/1275323/5452702-part-2-insight-
into-two-care-leavers-education-experience

 A webinar that Paul and Siobhan did together during the
pandemic on the 'art of analysis' can be viewed at
https://youtu.be/MwqqgJqxMus

 A video which Paul created of his artwork entitled 'Labels are
for Tins not People' can be viewed at
https://youtu.be/htM2f4Me3JA

In loving memory of Paul Yusuf McCormack

(25/01/1963 - 15/01/2021)